*Honest Talk about What
Makes a Partnership Last*

Marriage *for a* Lifetime

Floyd & Harriett Thatcher

Harold Shaw Publishers
Wheaton, Illinois

Previously published as *Long-Term Marriage: A Search for the Ingredients of a Lifetime Partnership*

Grateful acknowledgment is made to Marilee Zdenek for permission to use her poem in chapter eight from *God Is a Verb* by Marilee Zdenek and Marge Champion (Waco, TX: Word, 1974, p. 67).

ISBN 0-87788-505-2

Cover design by David LaPlaca

Edited by Mary Horner

Library of Congress Cataloging-in-Publication Data

Thatcher, Floyd W.
    Marriage for a lifetime : honest talk about what makes a partnership
  last / Floyd and Harriett Thatcher.
      p. cm.
    Rev. ed. of: Long term marriage. Waco, Tex. : Word Books, ©1980.
    Includes bibliographical references.
    ISBN 0-87788505-2 (paper)
    1. Marriage—United States. I. Thatcher, Harriett. II. Thatcher, Floyd W.
  Long term marriage. III. Title.
  HQ734.T38 1995
  306.81—dc20
                               95-34826
                                  CIP

---

02 01 00 99 98 97 96 95

10 9 8 7 6 5 4 3 2 1

To all of you
who opened up your homes to us
and freely shared feelings and experiences
from your married lives.

Contents

Acknowledgments

Our thanks to:

Wayne Oates, Jack Balswick, and Earl Koile for their affirmation and wise counsel throughout each stage of our study and writing.

Bruce Larson, Keith Miller, and Lloyd Ogilvie for invaluable advice and encouragement and for the many helpful suggestions which have kept us on target.

The select group of professional men and women who assisted us in making contact with the persons who were interviewed and whose stories are important to this book.

All of those people in the helping professions who gave professional advice and who shared of their time freely with us.

Pat Wienandt, our sensitive editor, whose help and guidance gave clarity to our writing.

Betty Lusk, for her typing and retyping of the manuscript.

For the Reader

We believe in marriage. We side with the overwhelming majority of people, even in today's society, who plan to get married, who hope to stay married, and who long for a relationship that will carry them forward through the years to enriching experiences and fulfillment as couples and as families. We also believe that marriage has not gone out of date in spite of the cataclysmic changes of one kind or another that have shaken our society's foundations over the last thirty years or so.

But young couples soon find that staying married and being happy about it isn't all that easy when it comes down to living through the day-to-day routines of maintaining the home, fulfilling the demands of job or profession, and confronting the confusing realities of rearing children. And as if that isn't enough, there is growing indication that staying married into, through, and beyond the midlife years is increasingly difficult. The burgeoning statistics of separation and divorce for couples married twenty or more years strike fear and anxiety into our hearts. At the same time, most of us are intimately aware that many marriages exist in a climate of bickering and tension, while others have become too tired and dull for anything except an apathetic relationship that places few demands on either partner as each goes his or her own way.

Late twentieth-century prophets of gloom and doom seem to find meaning by concentrating on the bad news. After all, it is threats of war, shady politics, acts of violence and crime, and ruptured human relationships that seem to make the best copy for the evening television news or the morning paper. But through our own experience and through observing other marriages, we have come to believe that not only is long-term marriage possible for two people who both want it that way, but that the relationship can grow and develop into a lively, loving, stimulating, adventuresome, and sexually exciting way of life as long as a couple lives.

It was this belief that put into motion our *search for the ingredients of a lifetime partnership.* The experiences of the many people we talked with during our three years of research verified our own feelings that there are no easy answers or quick solutions or pat formulas. We agree more firmly now than ever with Dorothy Samuel, who wrote in her book *Love, Liberation, and Marriage:* "Good marriages develop; they are fashioned out of long hours of doubt and despair and adjustment and compromise." This has been true for us as we have come to see that marriage is a constant movement—-we never arrive but are always in the process of becoming.

Our search took us into intimate and lengthy structured conversations with more than fifty married couples and with seventeen divorced persons, all of whom had been married at least twenty years. You will meet them through the "scenes" and comments throughout this book. The people in the "scenes" are real. All of the names and places, except one, have been changed to protect the privacy of the persons involved.

As we talked intimately with the people who agreed to share their experiences with us, our minds continually reflected back over the more than fifty years of our own married life. These personal flashbacks, thoughts, and feelings are also an integral part of this book. There's both hilarity and heartbreak in some of the episodes. It has been scary at times to express our feelings and share stories from our own marriage. But as we relived those experiences and the lessons learned, we have gained fresh courage and insight for the rest of our pilgrimage.

In preparation for this slightly revised new edition of our book, we have included a chapter on "Marriage and Retirement." Generally speaking we have restricted ourselves in this section to our own reactions and experiences as we have recently begun working our way into what it means to have a fulfilling marriage in the retirement years. We certainly don't consider ourselves authorities on how a lifetime marriage can handle the many changes that accompany retirement. But it is our hope that our experiences can be useful to couples either in the early stages of preparing for retirement or who are already in this time of their life.

We are keenly aware of the fact that there are certain aspects of the marriage experience we may have touched on lightly or not at all. Our purpose has not been to write a comprehensive, data-laden textbook on marriage. Rather, it was our intention to stay closely to the responses and feelings of our interviewees and to our own experiences, and to relate those experiences in a way that will solicit thought and response by people about to be married and by married couples of any age. We invite you to share in our experiences as you read these pages individually, as a couple, or within a small group setting.

Floyd and Harriett Thatcher
Waco, Texas
1995

Chapter One

What Ever Happened to Marriage?

> *It is quite clear that neither courses nor counseling will suffice in the face of our present widespread breakdown of marriage. We need a new moral contagion, one which brings about a change in deep-seated attitudes.*   Paul Tournier

It had been a good day. Things had gone well. And my feelings of well-being had received a boost when an author friend finally agreed to do his next book with the publishing firm I was associated with. I started home from the office and decided to take the longer, scenic route. Actually, I had a choice of three ways to go home—each fits a different mental attitude. But that day the scenic route which winds around by the edge of the lake fit my ebullient mood.

As I drove along and absorbed the beauty of the lake, the sun—a golden, shimmering ball, just beginning to dip below the gently rolling hills—cast a wavy ribbon of fire-like color across the water. The scattered cloud-wisps reflected a brilliant red-orange and stood out in sharp relief against the blue sky. The trees and underbrush which covered the hills were a lush green because of earlier summer rains.

The beauty of the late afternoon enhanced my feelings of well-being further, and by the time I wheeled around the corner into my driveway and carport, I was on an emotional high. But as I burst through the back door, I sensed something was not right. Missing were the usual kitchen noises—rattling pans or dishes—which, as a rule, accompany dinner preparations. Instead I found Harriett in the family room, sitting on the divan with a puzzled and somber look on her face. And rather than the usual warm and alive kiss I always looked forward to, I received a perfunctory peck that was about as stirring as a greeting from one's sister.

Obviously something was wrong, and my spirits had already begun to sag.

"What's wrong? What did I do?"

"No, that's not it," she responded. "We got some bad news today, and I'm just floored." And with that she handed me a letter. It was from Elisabeth, a childhood friend that she had kept in close touch with over the years. I read with amazement the bitter words which told of the breakup of her marriage with Allan. We had always thought their marriage was solid enough to survive almost any crisis. But there it was—Allan had moved out, said he was fed up with their marriage of twenty-nine years, wanted to be free from it all. And Elisabeth had filed for divorce.

With that, the successes of the day and the beauty of the ride home were forgotten and lost. We sat talking and wondering about it all for several hours. Twilight slipped into darkness but neither of us moved to turn on a lamp. Dinner was forgotten, but it didn't matter because we weren't hungry. We were bewildered by the questions which raced through our minds. *Why? What went wrong? How could this happen?* We were hurt and puzzled and a little afraid.

To be sure, this wasn't the first marriage breakup among our friends and acquaintances, but it was closer to home than the others—and the least expected. We weren't blind to what seemed to be the growing instability of marriages the last few years. But we were nonplussed by the apparent increase in the collapse of long-term marriages—those relationships of at least twenty years.

Changes in American family patterns were the subject of articles in almost every magazine. And we had recently been astonished by the statistics which indicated that the "typical American family" of past years—with a wage-earning husband, a homemaker wife, and two children—is now represented by only 7 percent of the families in the United States. A firsthand awareness of these changes had contributed to our growing feelings of insecurity, but the breakup of Elisabeth's marriage obsessed our thinking for days. We said little to each other at first about the enigmatic tug of war that was going on in our minds.

Could It Happen to Us?

It soon became clear through our discussions together that we were both wrestling with the same concerns. Harriett remembers: "For a time the old scary feelings crept into my thoughts that if this could happen to Elisabeth and Allan, it might also happen to Floyd and me. This same anxiety had produced a cold sweat and knots in my stomach every time we had heard over the years of friends and acquaintances whose marriages had failed.

"I had to test these fears with Floyd and was relieved to learn that, in his way, he was experiencing the same kind of disquieting fear and anxiety. And as we worked through our fears, we came to see that this was not a destructive reaction. Rather, it forced us to pause and reflect on our own relationship, and we were able to reaffirm our commitment.

"But we were both haunted by the same questions: What kinds of things lead to marriage breakup? Could this possibly happen to us even yet? How can two people who've lived together and slept together and made love come to the place where they can throw the whole thing over?"

We agreed that we would try to find some answers to these disturbing questions, and we began a firsthand search through personal interviews and study. Four years later, after thousands of miles of traveling, over one hundred personal interviews, and agonizing birth pangs, this book was born.

We understand, of course, that it is not the last word about why some marriages hold together and others don't. But these pages do represent the thoughts and the feelings—both hurts and joys—of the many people who have shared with us their awareness of the puzzling changes that are occurring in marriage and family life today. Some of the people we interviewed were divorced but most were still married. All had been married for more than twenty years. Some had hope for their own marriages. Others were pessimistic enough to believe that the radical shifts in marriage and family life over the past thirty to fifty years signal a disastrous breakdown in traditional values from which there seems little chance of recovery.

Out of these discussions we discovered fresh insights which have resulted in hours of conversation between Harriett and me about our own relationship—the kind of healthy self-examination we believe can enrich the experience of any couple, no matter how long they have been married. This should not be confused with a destructive and masochistic navel-gazing exercise whereby every flaw is examined and aired. Rather, we feel that by hearing of other people's experiences we can gain helpful insights that lead to positive communication about our own relationships.

In looking back over the more than fifty years of our own marriage, we find little similarity between who and what we were on our wedding day and the kind of people we have become. For us, it all started out one hot Sunday afternoon in Ventura, California. Following a honeymoon of absorbing the sights and smells and sounds of San Francisco's busy streets, jammed with bumper-to-bumper traffic and the ringing clang of cable cars, wandering wide-eyed through the exotic shops along China Town's Grant Street, and roaming arm in arm through Golden Gate Park, we settled down in our little rented duplex. Our daily work and routines were packed with new experiences. The responsibilities of marriage were still scary, but the adventure and excitement soothed our anxiety.

So, with the help of an adequate job, social acceptance, and a rewarding church relationship, we set out to model, as best we understood it, the correct marriage lifestyle. Our naivete knew no bounds and our sophomoric understanding of life was outrageous; but, happily, we didn't know it at the time.

During those days "respectable" couples didn't get divorces. The sexual escapades of civic or religious leaders in our town were hushed up while the respectability of their marriages was maintained behind a tight-lipped and steely-eyed facade. Few people lived together unless they had made their "till death do us part" commitment before a minister or judge. And, at least in our town, high school girls who got pregnant were considered outcasts. Of course we knew there was a lot of behind-the-scenes playing around—but not by "nice folks."

The Shock of Change

Certainly marriage and family life have undergone cataclysmic changes and innovations since we were married. This is true of virtually every area in modern society. Our nation's entry into space in the 1960s thrust us into a period of unprecedented change that has altered drastically the way we think and act. Peter Drucker offered an awesome pronouncement in that same year, stating that anyone who graduated from college in the 1970s and beyond would have to retrain at least twice during his or her lifetime.[1] The technological advances in the 1980s and 1990s have continued to accelerate at a breathtaking pace in a way that further validates Dr. Drucker's mind-stretching prophecy.

Now, to those of us old enough to even barely remember World War II and the DC-3 airplane, these fast-paced changes in the norms of marriage and family life have often left us bewildered and unsure of ourselves. In recent years we have been bombarded with a plethora of statistics and articles, whose sources range from the United States Bureau of the Census to a combination of professional and lay reporters in magazines and newspapers.

Paul Glick and Arthur Norton, both from the U.S. Bureau of the Census, report:

> The United States has one of the highest marriage rates—and the highest divorce rate—among the world's industrialized countries during recent years. . . . For persons 35 to 54 years old, the proportion of persons currently divorced went up by one-third between 1970 and 1975. . . . Close to two million unrelated men and women not married to each other are currently sharing living quarters.[2]

Writing in 1993, Dr. Norval D. Glenn of the University of Texas validates the Glick and Norton reports:

> Over the past three decades there has been a period of substantial changes in the institution of marriage in the U.S. The divorce rate doubled from 1965 to

1975, increased more slowly through the late 1970s, and leveled off in the 1980s, but at such a high level that almost two-thirds of the marriages entered into in recent years are expected to end in divorce or separation.[3]

To compound the shock to our traditional values, teenage pregnancy has skyrocketed in spite of the pill or easy access to condoms in the supermarket. And "out-of-wedlock births have increased substantially, so that one-fourth of all births now are to unmarried mothers."[4] At the same time, young people in their twenties, financially pressed, are reported to be flocking back to a rent-free, private room and bath in their parents' homes, with mother performing cooking and maid services and father footing the bill for the day-to-day amenities.

Some years ago, psychologist and columnist Dr. Joyce Brothers stated that marriage is a "quiet hell" for about half of American couples, and that four of twelve marriages will probably end in divorce, while another six will become loveless, "utilitarian" relationships to protect children, property, shared careers, and other goals. And a study done in Detroit in the early 1960s by Doctors Blood and Wolfe indicated that only 6 percent of the wives interviewed were very satisfied with their marriages after twenty-two years of living with their husbands.[5]

A Brighter Side

But we believe it possible that this dreary litany is only part of the story. Many authorities estimate that over half of today's marriages do make it; ours has. Marriage is still the option preferred by most men and women. Dr. Glenn reports:

[The notion that marriage] is a moribund or dying institution is inconsistent with the fact that a large percentage of Americans say that having a happy marriage is one of the most important ... goals in their lives. About two-fifths of the respondents to the 1989 Massachusetts Mutual American Values Study indicated this was one of their most important values, and more than 90 percent said it was one of the most important or very important. Approximately three-fourths of the high school seniors studied by the Monitoring the Future Project at the University of Michigan in recent years have stated they definitely will marry, and the proportion has not declined.[6]

And we are beginning to hear rumblings that appear to signal disenchantment with the living-together-outside-of-marriage phenomenon that has struck bold headlines in recent years. We are hearing and reading about more and more couples who decide to marry after living together a few months or for several years. Why do they bother if this kind of lifestyle is completely satisfying and free from what some feel are the hypocrisies of vows not kept and a piece of paper signed by a minister or judge?

But living-together arrangements do not seem to give valid assurance of a trouble-free utopia to a couple, even though, in theory, a walk-out by one of the partners is supposed to be less complicated. Human emotions are lacerated, feelings are hurt, relationships are ruptured, whether or not vows have been formally made and official papers signed.

There is overriding indication, though, that the public acceptance and security that marriage affords provides the best basis for satisfying and lasting relationships. When we take all circumstances into consideration, there seems to be ample evidence that marriage offers the best opportunity for a secure, comfortable, and fulfilling relationship, both emotionally and spiritually.

More Questions

As we reflected on the miracle of marriage, several questions struggled for answers in our minds:

- Why do some marriages last? What is the glue that holds them together?
- Why do other marriages fail? What are the disruptive factors that lead to the breakdown of a marriage relationship with its pain and alienation?

And then we asked ourselves: Why has our marriage held together? After all, at eighteen and not quite twenty-one years old, we certainly weren't prepared for the drastic change from single to married life, including occupying one double bed. We were even less prepared for the sudden shift from what we then called heavy petting (and no intercourse) to the freedom of enjoying each other sexually, simply because the minister had said a few properly selected words and signed the marriage license. Before those words was the agony of sexual frustration and afterwards the bewilderment of fantasies not wholly fulfilled, at least at first. Then after a succession of years came the birth of our daughter, two major changes in profession, and two traumatic geographic uprootings with the accompanying cultural shock and emotional upheaval.

Nothing remains absolutely the same for long. People grow and change and change and grow. At twenty-seven and thirty we were different people from who we were at eighteen and twenty-one. And then at forty-two and forty-five our style had shifted drastically—we didn't think, eat, play, worship, or make love like we did at eighteen and twenty-one or twenty-seven and thirty. There has been an almost frightening yet exhilarating fluidity to our lives which leaves us more than a little breathless and at times a shade apprehensive. In 1970 Margaret Mead viewed the scene:

> No other generation has ever known, experienced, and struggled to incorporate such massive and rapid change—has watched while the sources of energy, the means of communication, the certainties of a known world, the limits of the explorable universe, the definition of humanity, and the fundamental imperatives of life and death have changed before their eyes. Adults today know more about change than any previous generation.[7]

And that was written before the dramatic changes of the 1970s, 1980s, and 1990s. Nevertheless, Dr. Mead's observations continue to be right on target.

Around 500 B.C. an exceptionally wise man, Heraclitus of Ephesus in Asia Minor, put it very well when he said that everything is flowing—one cannot enter twice into the same stream, for every moment the water changes.

Yes, our marital stream has done a lot of flowing, and so again we ask: Why have *we* made it against such heavy odds? Why do some make it while others don't? Is it because those who make it do everything right while others do everything wrong? We doubted it.

The Search for Answers

In trying to find some answers we talked with people who had been married for at least twenty years—some still were; others had agonized over the death of their marriage and the bitterness of divorce. From the East Coast to the

West Coast, the Midwest to the Southwest, we talked with people about why their marriages are holding or what they think led to failure.

What have we learned from these thousands of miles involving more than two hundred hours of questions and conversation about what makes good marriages work? That's what this book is all about. Many of our questions have found answers satisfactory to us, others are still a little gray, and some seem to defy any attempt at closure. One thing is certain: we haven't found the perfect couple, and we could not locate hard-and-fast, sure-bet rules for successful marriages. There doesn't seem to be an etched-in-stone decalogue for long-term marriage given to us amidst thunder and lightning on some distant mountain peak.

But we have discovered some green "go" lights and some red "stop" lights, along with an arresting succession of yellow "caution" lights; and have uncovered some characteristics of the glue that seems to be an essential ingredient of healthy, enriching, and lasting marriage. We believe that intriguing and helpful insights are gained from sharing in the experiences of other people. And in the process each of us can begin to arrive at a better understanding of the marriage adventure and be able to cope responsibly with the complexities of our own relationship.

Chapter Two

Why Did You Get Married?

A wedding is not a marriage. A wedding is only the beginning of an undertaking that may or may not, someday, develop into a marriage. What the couple have on their wedding day is not the key to a beautiful garden, but just a vacant lot and a few gardening tools.   David and Vera Mace

Scene 1—Phyllis and Ed

Phyllis Woodson sat facing us with her arms and legs both crossed, one leg bouncing up and down while her fingers drummed a staccato beat on the arm of her chair. Her forehead was creased in deep concentration, and her lips were pressed together in a thin line. Her eyes darted first from us to her husband, and then to the doorway, as if she half expected someone to violate our privacy any moment.

Why had Phyllis wanted to get married? Without any hesitation she snapped, "To get away from home." While her childhood home was outwardly respectable, it had evidently been a hell of rigidity, devoid of love expressed by either words or actions. Anything was better than that, so at nineteen she married Ed "to get away from it all."

Why had Ed married Phyllis? She was sexy—viewed from front or rear, going or coming. Sure they loved each other as best they understood the meaning of the word. But as far as Ed was concerned, their heavy petting, or making out or whatever you want to call it, had convinced

24

him that Phyllis was exactly what he wanted to come home to—and often.

Scene 2—Faye and Bill

It was on a Sunday afternoon in June that we made our way along a tranquil, magnolia-lined street in a southeastern town. The fragrance of honeysuckle weighted the warm afternoon air. Nestled in the pines, well back from the street, was a stately, white plantation-style home straight from *Gone with the Wind* except on a smaller scale. Here we met Faye and Bill Thomas, who received us with velvet dignity. Why had Faye and Bill gotten married twenty-seven years before?

To them, it seemed a strange question. With studied expression, Bill responded first: "I wanted a wife and home. Being single was fun for a while, but I got tired of that and wanted to settle down. Besides, down here, sooner or later everybody that matters gets married and settles down to a useful life. That's what my grandfather and daddy did, and it was just expected that I'd do the same."

In the meantime, Faye's face was a study in concentration, but after a rather long silence, she began, "I don't think I've ever thought about that before. When we got married Bill was twenty-four and I was twenty-one. For generations the women in my family had married young—and to strong men. I wanted someone to take care of me like my daddy had. Bill and I had known each other since the sixth grade and dated steadily through high school and college. Of course, there was the sex thing, and I'd been raised to wait. Well, we almost did."

Scene 3—Counseling Session

The scene shifts to the office of a marriage counselor friend of ours who told us this story which we've put in our own words.

The atmosphere in the room bristled with hostility. Three people sat facing each other—the couple was tense, obviously angry, and very uneasy. They were careful not to look at each other as their eyes roamed furtively around the room, resting now and then for brief moments on the marriage counselor.

After just a little encouragement from our friend, the dam seemed to break, and for forty-five minutes a steady stream of complaints gushed out into the room. She didn't feel loved. . . . He never complimented her . . . . She used sex to manipulate him into doing what she wanted. . . . She was always criticizing him and tearing him down. . . . He was quiet and withdrawn most of the time and wouldn't talk to her. . . . He harped at her for spending too much money. On and on it went.

Finally, the marriage counselor broke in, looked her straight in the eyes, and asked, "Why did you marry him in the first place?"

With only a moment's hesitation she responded, "I have asked myself that question several times lately, and I've just figured out what happened. During high school and college I was very popular. Most of the fellows fell for me at one time or another, but he didn't. This really hurt my pride. He became a challenge and an obsession, so I set out to seduce him and get him. I did, and after a time we legalized it all and got married. It's been a disaster ever since."

Scene 4—Ralph and Anne

It was one of those classic days in the Los Angeles basin that evoked strong feelings of nostalgia. Harriett and I found ourselves carried back to a time just a few months after we were married, when we had moved to this very community. In those days intricate freeway systems had not yet cut the ugly scars that now slash across once quiet and tranquil neighborhoods, and the word *smog* hadn't yet invaded our vocabulary.

But on this day the rugged San Gabriel Mountains stood out in bold relief against the blue sky; the noxious yellow haze which so frequently presses down on the city and smothers its exuberance had disappeared completely. The clear air made it seem as if we could reach out and touch the mountains even though the foothills were four miles from where we were on a little side street in suburbia, well away from the freeway's incessant hum. Clearly we were in a middle-class neighborhood. There was a depressing and monotonous sameness about the whole scene. The construction varied slightly, but not enough for even a faint hint of individuality. Similar landscaping marked every yard, and boundaries were clearly defined by prim white picket fences. It was as if the neighbors at the end of the block on each side of the street had designed their yards and that same design had, with minor changes, been copied and passed along.

Ralph and Anne Hartman lived in the middle of their block in a yellow stucco home with white trim. Bermuda grass carpeted the yard, and here and there was a shrub or small tree. The house was neat and orderly and plain. And it was apparent that the furnishings had been bought in stages, probably from a furniture discount house, with not much thought given to style.

Why had Ralph and Anne gotten married twenty-one years ago, when she was only seventeen and he was twenty? In a resigned and flat tone of voice, Anne's first reason tumbled out, "I was two months pregnant and scared. What would my parents think? My father was a strict, no-nonsense, rigid religious type who had always said he'd throw me out if I ever got into trouble, and I knew he meant it. As a child, I'd never measured up. Over and over again he let me know in a thousand ways that I was a disappointment to him. And it seemed that he paid attention to me only when he was mad about something. Now I had really blown it. And I knew my mother would go along with whatever he did—she always had knuckled under when his explosions rocked the house."

Throughout this rather breathless flow Ralph had been nodding in agreement. "It wasn't that Anne and I had played around a lot. Sure, we'd had our heavy moments, but somehow she always managed to keep things under control. This time, though, there was no stopping and we got caught.

"It wasn't long before I knew from the way she acted that something was wrong, and a few weeks later she told me she was pregnant. We were young and loved each other, so we ran off to Las Vegas one night and got married in one of those made-to-order wedding chapels. All hell broke loose when we got back, and Anne's father never did forgive us before he died. Guess our reason for getting married at that time wasn't so good, but we've sort of had to grow up together, and we were both dead set on proving to the old man that we could make it in spite of his self-righteous predictions that we'd fall on our faces. Then when he died, our patterns were pretty well set, and we've had a fairly comfortable life so far."

Scene 5—Sue

Sue Little lived on the edge of downtown St. Louis in a nondescript, gray wood frame house that was long overdue for a paint job. The grass in the front yard was overgrown, and the bottom step leading up to the porch was partially rotted. A neatly typed note told me the doorbell didn't work, so I knocked somewhat hesitantly on the weatherbeaten front door. I was almost immediately greeted by Sue—a slim, attractive, and neatly dressed lady in her mid-forties, with a figure that could well be the envy of a woman fifteen years younger.

We settled down for our interview in a couple of well-worn chairs and began to talk against the whir of two electric fans, one at each end of the room. It was a hot, muggy day, typical of St. Louis in July, and Sue explained that the air conditioner had just gone out. Before doing what obviously was a prearranged disappearing act, her teenage daughter brought us a couple of glasses of iced tea as a gesture of hospitality.

Sue's divorce had been final just a year, and the hurt, tinged by a shade of bitterness, showed through clearly. What had happened? Her husband of twenty-three years had walked out of their $100,000 suburban split-level home two years before and was now married to his twenty-seven-year-old secretary. Fortunately, Sue's early training had been as a dental assistant, so she was able to get a job rather easily, but she and her daughter had been forced to move into this low-cost housing soon after the divorce in order to make ends meet.

Why had Sue gotten married in the first place? "I was always sort of an idealistic girl who pictured myself as a homemaker and mother. Having a family was important to me, and I had a storybook concept of marriage. You know, the ideal man, the perfect husband, everything would be wine and roses while we had babies, raised our children, attended church occasionally, and then grew old together happily. Things had always come easy for me, and I just assumed they would go on that way.

"Roy was stable and had a fairly good paying job at the bank. While he hadn't advanced as fast as he thought he should, Roy did receive regular pay raises even though he was passed up for promotion a couple of times. I felt we were moving into middle age rather comfortably, and I don't think I was threatened too much by the passing years and the subtle changes in my figure.

"But then things began to happen and change. Roy seemed restless and uneasy. One day he decided to start jogging in an effort to get his flat stomach back. A little later he came home from a clothes-buying spree with a rather loud sports outfit and several pairs of jeans—quite a change from the suits and tailored slacks he'd always worn before. But it was a month or so later that I got my big shock—he drove home one afternoon in a shiny new red sports car. We really couldn't afford that kind of extravagance.

"Over the years we'd had the usual disagreements and arguments most couples have, but this time we had a real knock-down, drag-out fight. We argued and shouted through dinner, past the ten o'clock news, and finally exhausted, we gave up and went to bed. The next morning was the same. For two or three weeks the atmosphere thawed a little, but I knew things were different.

"Then one night Roy came in and abruptly announced that he'd had it; that he was going to leave for good and move in with his secretary. What for me had been a story-book marriage now came crashing down with paralyzing suddenness. I didn't want to go on living, but I had a teenage daughter to care for. So in the midst of my anger and depression, I set out to try to make it one day at a time."

Handling Our Reasons for Getting Married

As we listened to all these people talk about why they had gotten married years before, we realized how many had pinned their hopes on unrealistic preconceptions about marriage and on impossible dreams about how a husband and wife actually communicate and love. And while the conditions of our own backgrounds are quite different, we can identify in many ways with the feelings expressed in a *Family Weekly* article, in which Italian actress Sophia Loren was quoted: "I started life with only one possession, the only valuable possession a slum child can have—her dreams. . . . I am as insecure today as I ever was. Anything any of us ever have, we can lose."

Although it is true that we can lose many things—even our closest loved one—Harriett and I feel, after our research, that there are securities couples can have which cannot be taken away, and which act as a bonding glue at the deepest levels to hold us together. *These securities cluster around an honest and shared awareness of deeply ingrained value systems gained from aligning ourselves with the unseen but deeply felt rhythms of life.* While *we* would say these rhythms come from God, others might not. But in either case, these rhythms are a part of the rubric of things beyond ourselves which stand as a continuing challenge in face of the pessimism of so many couples about marriage.

Kathy Lowry gives us an optimistic word in a *Family Weekly* article when she writes, "Indeed, marriage is suddenly making a comeback—and not only by hip suburbanites who earlier had opted for living together as an alternate lifestyle." She cites figures released by the Department of Health, Education, and Welfare stating that the number of marriages had increased from 1.5 to 2.1 million annually in the 1960s and 1970s. And Ms. Lowry adds, "Honeymoons, too, are up; 98 percent of all couples are taking them—and to traditional places at that."[1]

But if a large percentage of these new marriages are going to be intact ten or twenty years from now, our study—and our experience—indicates these couples will be wise to reflect honestly on their reasons for getting married in the first place. And irrespective of what those reasons might have been, they will need to work together at building a caring relationship for the future. Certainly,

31

there is one key question that confronts all of us at the time we get married, and then recurs at each stage of life thereafter: *How can we handle unreal expectations in the drama of marriage?* And this leads to a second question: *How can we learn the secret of setting realistic expectations for our marriage and family relationship—expectations that we can build on for personal and marital enrichment?*

Chapter Three

What Did You Expect?

> *Your own wishes and dreams must coincide with
> your mate's and be within the realm of attainment
> for you—neither beneath or beyond you. For if
> they are not realistically built and mutually
> carried out, they lead to frustration and
> stagnation in marriage rather than to emotional
> comfort.*   David Abrahamsen

"I think I expected too much; that there wouldn't be any
conflict, everything would always work out."

"I believed that the honeymoon would just go on forever."

"I expected to have the last word in marriage. That's the
way it was in my parents' home. I had a rude awakening
when my wife made it clear she wasn't about to buy that
approach."

"I believed that marriage would be like a storybook
romance, and I never could accept the fact that it might not
be that way. When it never came together, I got bitter and
cynical and just gave up trying."

"I thought we wouldn't have any fights, that we could
always talk things out, and that love could overcome
anything. But I soon learned that was unrealistic."

"I expected it to be like it was in my mother's and
father's case—he was the boss, not just a little but all the
way. I felt this was the way it was supposed to be, so when
my husband wasn't like that, I was critical of him for not

being as assertive as I thought he should be. That kind of killed my respect for him."

"I think the significant thing I expected was that I would be protected. I was terribly afraid of the dark, and after we were married if Don went out even on a quick errand and I was left alone in the apartment, I sat facing the door and never moved until he came back. I was really looking for protection and someone who would be very warm, considerate, and totally trustworthy."

"I was lonely at home before marriage, and I thought marriage would take care of that. It didn't; I felt lonely during much of the time we were married, and after he walked out, it just got worse."

"I expected sort of a fairy-tale type of thing. I never pictured us having any problems. But the difference between fairy tale and reality is pretty drastic. As a whole it has been very satisfying, but there have been some bad times too. I think our marriage has lasted this long because we've worked out solutions to most of the major problems."

Unrealistic Expectations

In the business world there is a well-worn phrase which is often tossed around loosely by the would-be chic who hope to impress with jargon: "What about the *bottom line?*" or "How does this affect the *bottom line?*" This tired and overworked cliché arouses all sorts of feelings in me, not because I believe profit isn't a legitimate goal, but because frequently, I've heard it used as a cover-up for a lack of creative and innovative thinking. But to capitalize on this familiar imagery, when it comes right down to the "bottom line" of marriage, we feel that most of us enter into this relationship with grossly unrealistic expectations, or no definable expectations at all.

Unbelievable as it may be, the truth is that all too many of us move into marriage with an insect's-eye view of what it is all about. What can be the most vital and rewarding of all human relationships is sold short and often left to chance because many of us, whether we were married in 1940, 1970, or 1990, are unprepared to interpret what kind of a future we should expect.

Should we expect a storybook marriage? a romantic relationship? no disagreements? a marriage like our parents'? an endless honeymoon? no conflicts? A variety of conditions, events, and experiences influence our expectations, but probably none are as strong as the impressions passed along from our parents and grandparents, and from one generation to the next.

Cutting corners in the marriage relationship for short-term success may well result in a subtle and crippling succession of seemingly right achievements which, in the long term, can spell disaster to the marriage. For example, an ambitious husband with abnormally high business expectations and money-making goals can so submerge himself in his profession that he has no time or energy left to work at building a solid, person-to-person, growing relationship with his wife. He rationalizes this single-minded preoccupation by insisting that someday his wife and family will have and enjoy the comfortable, good things of life that money can buy. But in the process he has lost sight of the fact that solid human values and deep, loving relationships cannot thrive on either neglect or apathy. This is not to denigrate the healthy desire to provide well for the comforts and good things for one's wife and family; but if this is done at the expense of time and energy devoted to the building and growth of the marriage relationship, the "bottom line" may well produce a sterile and brittle lifestyle—a shortcut to disaster.

Another example is the wife and mother who is absorbed in the delicate effort of juggling a career, either out of necessity or choice, with the pressures of home and family. The stress of this balancing act can exact a tremendous physical and emotional toll. Or there is the ambitious wife with inflated expectations to be the "superwife," devoting all of her energies to achieve social acceptance as a means of helping her husband succeed. In both situations, in spite of right motives, the couple is likely to be deprived of needed time in which to share their innermost thoughts and become involved in the kinds of activities that blend two human spirits together into a deep, feeling relationship. Goals and expectations can run afoul, and the marriage can end up with an empty "bottom line."

We see now that in our own preparation for marriage, we weren't any different from the vast majority of couples. Harriett remembers, "I don't believe my early expectations were very realistic. I just thought you got married and life would unfold in a beautiful pattern. I had no concept of anything being so difficult about it. I don't recall the when, what, or why of our first quarrel, but I do remember being utterly shocked and crushed—that just wasn't supposed to happen."

And as for me, my social and educational background hadn't prepared me to expect a great deal; the capacity to dream came later. So I muddled into it with sort of a day-at-a-time attitude, convinced that our marriage would probably work, but with no idea of what it might take to make it happen. There were no great dreams for the future except if "I kept my nose to the grindstone" and worked hard, everything would probably come out all right.

Looking back now, I can see how we fit the indictment Eugene Ionesco made in a speech at the opening of the

Salzburg Fair in 1972: "People are going round in circles in the cage of their planet, because they have forgotten they can look up to the sky. . . . Because all we want is to live, it has become impossible for us to live." In those early years we had a pretty dreary and uncreative approach to a deeply significant relationship, and we lived in a beige world. We were, in truth, caught in "the cage of our planet," without the capability of looking beyond the involvement of the moment toward the exciting horizons of life. But there have been a good many dreams and a world of changes since then. While we've not always succeeded, we've tried desperately to avoid the trap of cutting the kinds of relational corners that would produce an empty bottom line on our marriage balance sheet.

In a *Family Weekly* article, Mary Susan Miller tells this story:

> On their fifteenth wedding anniversary Nancy exploded at her husband Mack, "Do you know what I really want you to give me?" She hurled the hiking boots he had bought her across the floor and yelled, "A divorce!" Her husband was stunned. He had thought their marriage was great!
>
> Eight months, one marriage counselor, and a thousand dollars later, they had begun to see what was wrong. Mack had spent fifteen years turning Nancy into his best friend, the buddy he hadn't had since his war days. Nancy had spent those same fifteen years longing for her husband to love and baby her as her father had done years earlier.[1]

What a waste! Fifteen years of being insensitive to each other's signals. Why? And more important, what could they have done to make it different?

Sharing Dreams versus Creeping Separateness

We have come to suspect strongly that *dreams and shared expectations, discussed and talked about, are some of the ingredients from which durable and lasting marriages are made.* While it is probably true that most couples move into the marriage relationship with only a vague notion of what to really expect, there's usually a resiliency to those early weeks, months, and years as a couple seeks to adjust to one another and share openly hopes and dreams with each other.

During those early years "we begin to build what behaviorists call 'success experiences.' In most marriages, shared goals come quite naturally during the first years."[2] For some couples those early success experiences may include putting out the down payment on a new home, buying a second car, or taking a trip to the Orient with stops in Tokyo, Taipei, and Hong Kong. For others, success experiences are measured by starting a family and acquiring such comforts for home and play as a new bedroom suite, a microwave oven, or even a set of Hogan golf clubs. It is this common pulling together in the struggle to fulfill new expectations that makes for the building of the relationship.

But then after a few years, a curious thing frequently happens—the excitement sags, stars begin to fade, inner fires die down and only flicker spasmodically. The realization slowly dawns that even in the midst of those early success experiences there was the haunting and very human feeling that they were too good to last. Father Chuck Gallagher feels that, from our early childhood, many of our models for marriage planted the notion that relationships usually grow stale and dull: "Even though we might hope the glow would last, we don't expect it to. When the focus begins to shift from each other to the activities of everyday life, the couple in love resign themselves to being ordinary people."[3]

Ordinary living spawns dullness, and dullness usually gives way to boredom, and boredom breeds that "quiet hell" Dr. Joyce Brothers says plagues about half of American marriages. Expectations, hopes, and dreams are no longer shared. There is a deadness of feeling, a flatness, a drifting apart. Sheldon Vanauken diagnosed this paralyzing condition as "creeping separateness." He writes:

> The killer of love is creeping separateness. . . . Taking love for granted, especially after marriage. Finding separate interests. "We" turning into "I." Self. Self-regard: what I want to do. Actual selfishness only a hop away. . . . The failure of love might seem to be caused by hate or boredom or unfaithfulness with a lover; but those were results. First came the creeping separateness; the failure behind the failure.[4]

Lest we be misread at this point, it is important to understand that we do not believe the answer to the deadly creeping separateness Vanauken pictures is that either a husband or wife completely submerges individual personal identity within the other. Rather, the blending of a couple in marriage is the coming together of two souls at the deepest levels, a blending of what Carl Jung calls the *psyche*, the "thought, feeling and behavior, both conscious and unconscious."[5]

Scene 1—Bob and Lois

Bob Wilson was a highly successful internist. He exuded an aura of studied elegance that was more than a little intimidating. Most of his patients came from upper-class Los Angeles and Beverly Hills neighborhoods. Lois Wilson was chic and stylish, and obviously very comfortable and at ease in their fashionable Bel Air home. Still, there was a sort of papier-mâché quality to the entire setting.

We hadn't been there long before we wondered why the Wilsons had agreed to talk to us. Their responses to our questions appeared to have a hollow ring, and they seemed quite casual about their lack of common interests. By their own admission, Bob and Lois seldom went out together except to keep up appearances at society or civic functions. About the only time Lois showed much spirit in our conversation was when she complained about Bob's total preoccupation with his profession, which involved long hours away from home most of the time. And, according to Lois, Bob's only other interest was his regular Sunday morning golf game—apparently only a torrential downpour kept him off the Bel Air Club course. It was a frosty and cheerless scene.

In response to our question about why they got married and about their early expectations and dreams, they both brightened a bit and admitted to a white-hot love affair and to early dreams of a full and exciting life together. And then Lois, with a hint of wistfulness in her voice, said, "But we sort of drifted apart gradually. Bob was submerged in his thing, striving to make good in that medical jungle he likes so well, to be the best, to attract wealthy patients. I got involved with the Junior League, the symphony auxiliary, and Planned Parenthood. It seemed like we saw each other at odd moments and never really talked."

They didn't say it in so many words, but we got the picture: their dreams had faded. They had stopped trying and settled into a dull and lifeless marriage routine. There was no apparent warmth between them and certainly no emotional support. Lois enjoyed her role as the wife of an affluent and popular doctor, and Bob was proud of his wife's sexy good looks and stylish charm. She was just the kind of wife he needed to project the right image to his patients and peers. Theirs appeared to be a semi-harmonious, no-common-ground marriage. They went their separate ways, did their own thing, and for selfish reasons made the relationship work.

Scene 2—Paul and Martha

Just a couple of nights later we visited Paul and Martha Hoving in Van Nuys. Paul was assistant manager of a neighborhood grocery store, and Martha worked as a secretary at their church office. They lived in an ordinary house in an ordinary neighborhood, and they wore ordinary clothes and drove an ordinary car, but we soon discovered they weren't ordinary people.

There was a softness and warmth about Paul and Martha which seemed to reach out and take us in. And their conversation throughout the evening was liberally flavored with comments and stories which told of their interest in other people and what was going on around them. It was clear, too, that a deep faith in God was the agreed-upon foundation for every expression of their lives, including marriage. Home and church were the terminals from which flowed a network of relationships and activities that provided meaning and purpose for them.

What about their expectations? "Oh, we had them," Martha responded. "We never had even one serious argument during the two years we went together. Some little ones, yes, but it was so much fun making up that we soon forgot what had caused them in the first place—we thought it would always be like that. And like several of our friends, we did our share of fantasizing about a large home in the hills with a panoramic view of San Fernando valley, a swimming pool, and a yard that looked like a page from *Better Homes and Gardens* magazine. We thought our marriage would be just one string of happy experiences, including plenty of money to travel and to do the fun things we enjoy. But I guess our expectations weren't too realistic way back then. We've worked at our marriage, and I'm very grateful for the life we have."

Paul interrupted, "It hasn't always been easy, but we've kept reassuring each other—not just now and then, but every day, day in and day out. We've done a lot of things wrong, but most of the time we have been able to talk through our misunderstandings."

They had made it for a little more than twenty-two years. And from all that we saw and heard, they've got many more years ahead of them.

A Close Look at Ourselves

In talking later about Bob and Lois and Paul and Martha, Harriett and I reflected back over our own marriage, as we have so often lately. We recalled that at first our energies were poured into making it from one weekly paycheck to the next weekly paycheck, and then after a time it was from the first of the month to the fifteenth and to the first again. Along with that were my day-to-day dreams of meeting sales goals. Those dreams persisted even in my sleep. More than once in the middle of the night Harriett wakened me as I was forcefully giving a sales presentation.

At the time I didn't understand what was happening to me, but I have since come to realize that a powerful stream of energy and purpose was flowing from my conscious mind into my subconscious mind. And as this energy and determination then moved back from the unconscious to the conscious with action-directed purpose, I was rewarded with a succession of promotions which brought the success I'd been pushing for.

But then a strange uneasiness began to haunt me. Was this what life was all about? Did we want to stay on this merry-go-round, fighting our way from one horse to the next one up ahead? And then when we got bored with the circular horse-chasing routine, were we merely interested in changing the game to some variation of musical chairs—ruthlessly trying to grab a chair and cut someone else out of the game?

After months of sharing our deepest feelings the decision was made: we wanted out of the game. There had to be a better and more satisfying way. So we sold everything but a few personal belongings, and I went back to school in the Pacific Northwest.

Our early expectations, such as they were, were shattered. Harriett worked. I worked, along with taking twenty unit hours of classwork every semester. There was no time or energy to dream on a day-to-day basis, and certainly no time for life-dreams even if we had known how to dream then. The shift from junior executive to student was ego-shattering for me, and our meager income covered only the barest of necessities. We had no time for each other and little time for our daughter. But somehow we survived, and after three years we were ready to begin a new life.

Later when we became aware of the importance of having and sharing expectations, of dreaming and sharing dreams and of renewing them constantly, of putting feet to our spiritual faith, a whole new world began to open up before us as persons and as a married couple. Slowly, too slowly, we began to see *that our expectations and dreams were meant for far bigger things than we had understood before—a quality of life, a creative awareness of our personhood, a practical tool for enriching our marriage.*

As we listened to our hearts and read books insatiably, we began to understand a little better the idea expressed by Alex Osborn, "When we look forward to something we want to come true, and strongly believe that it will come true, we can often *make* ourselves *make* it come true."[6]

The Power of Affirmation

And it was about that time that we began to learn a little about what for us was a marriage-changing, life-changing principle. We discovered *the strength and power of personal affirmation—the conscious feeding of positive and creative feelings and information into our subconscious minds on a daily basis.*

We came to understand that in large measure we are what we are because of the information, the impressions, the feelings, the attitudes that have been "programmed" into our subconscious minds over the years even from young childhood. So many of us have, in Transactional Analysis language, "played tapes," consciously or unconsciously, which cause us to think negatively and critically; to think small; to become inordinately preoccupied with the present; to have a low opinion of ourselves; to believe that we really don't deserve true happiness or the good things in life; to always expect the worst from ourselves and other people; to play it safe and never take risks; to be obsessed with a fear of failure.

Theodore Roosevelt painted a vivid picture of the sterility of a certain style of life when he said, "Far better it is to dare mighty things, to win glorious triumphs, even though checkered by failure, than to rank with those poor spirits who neither enjoy much nor suffer much, because they live in the gray twilight that knows not victory or defeat."

And Reuel Howe has helped us see and confront what can happen so easily:

> There is always the tragic discrepancy between the life we feel and the life we can express, between the dream and its realization, between the brilliance of a thought conceived and its articulation. There is always

the cooling down of the original flame. The results of our efforts to express ourselves are so disappointing as compared with the glory and promise of our visions that we begin sometimes to doubt the vision also. When this happens, we begin to water down hopes and settle for smaller goals.[7]

Harriett and I realized that our hopes had become watered down by an unconscious acceptance of expediency, and that we had unintentionally drifted into an acceptance of the mediocrity and complacency that seemed to be the style of our times—all of this in spite of the learning experiences years before in business and school. But even though we might take two steps forward and slide back one, we vowed never again to accept (for long) the ordinary and the dull, in our personal lives or in our marriage relationship.

Dr. Viktor Frankl, a writer who has been a strong influence in our thinking, says, "It is a peculiarity of man that he can only live by looking to the future."[8] And over a century ago Henry David Thoreau, as he contemplated the movements within the world of persons from the shores of Walden Pond, seemed to catch the spirit of this life-changing truth when he wrote: "I learned this, at least, by my experiment: that if one advances confidently in the direction of his dreams, and endeavors to live the life which he has imagined, he will meet with success unexpected in common hours."

How it Works for Us

Let's get back to the technique of affirmation. How can it work, and what difference can it make? We learned that a steady habit of making creative and positive affirmations is a powerful force for changing attitudes and behavior in all of life, including marriage. But to be effective an affirmation must be worded, we came to see, as if the statement being made is reality, is true, now. The idea is based upon the belief that the unconscious mind, of itself, does not distinguish between an existing situation or fact and an imagined situation or fact.

For example, suppose that I have a habit of putting Harriett down, of being picky and critical of her, and of chipping away at her accomplishments. (This doesn't happen to be the case, but it does illustrate the point.) As I become aware of this destructive attitude and habit, I begin to understand the reality that it is crippling our relationship and is devastating to her as a person. Then I sit down to write an affirmation which I repeat several times a day until the deepest recesses of my mind have absorbed the message. That affirmation might read something like this: "Harriett is a warm, loving person with good ideas which are thought through carefully and are well expressed. I value her as a person and am glad she's my wife."

This affirmation is stating a positive fact in the feelings compartment of my subconscious mind. And as it is repeated four, five, six times a day, day in and day out, the subconscious mind starts to send back warm and positive messages to my conscious mind. And at that point we begin to act out those positive messages, and our thinking patterns and behavior start to conform to the positive affirmation. No longer is there room for negative, critical thoughts that breed put-downs, or for carping criticisms that chip away at another's sense of self-worth and can sour a relationship.

But it is in the expectations and dreams department of our lives that the principle of affirmation can be most exciting and effective. About the time we were beginning to discover this life-changing concept some thirty years ago, we had just awakened to the fact that our lives had become rather humdrum and were regulated on a daily basis by a sterile and boring routine. We seemed to be moving aimlessly in a sort of gray twilight. From Monday through Friday we did the same things at the same time as if on cue. Each morning we joined the thousands of other cars on the freeway, inching along to our office. And at night it was a repeat performance in reverse—fourteen miles and one hour each way. Night after night and every weekend we did the same things, with rarely any variation. We had become completely predictable and hadn't actually excelled a whole lot in the growing process. Determined to break out of this mold, we started to concentrate on bringing about some change in our lives. We began to dream in pictures.

During one of our family discussions, I expressed the idea that it might be fun to have a small mountain cabin somewhere in the San Bernardino Mountains—a place we could enjoy on weekends and vacations. Since we had just moved into a new home high up in the hills above Monterey Park, to take on the added financial burden of a mountain cabin seemed out of the question. But we decided to give it a try.

Together, we wrote out our affirmation on two cards— one for Harriett's purse and one for my shirt pocket. It read something like this: "We enjoy spending weekends in our mountain cabin nestled under tall pines high up in the San Bernardino Mountains." Several times a day, in moments of quiet, each of us, wherever we were, would repeat that dream-affirmation. I could close my eyes and picture a brown-shingled redwood cabin with green shutters perched on the side of a hill. It wasn't too big and it wasn't too small, and I could actually smell the pines in the thin mountain air.

Finally one day, three months later, we drove up into those mountains as we had done so many times before. But this time it wasn't the same. And after several hours we found it—a cabin not too different from what we'd been picturing, and it had a breathtaking view of the surrounding mountains. It was encircled by towering pines and, even though it wasn't very large, it had all the comforts of home. While it was more than we could afford at the time, it wasn't an impossible undertaking. We set about to work out the details, and in a few days it all came together with the aid of a hungry realtor and our helpful banker. And so began a new adventure at Running Springs, altitude 6,000 feet. Our dream had taken definite shape.

Elbert Hubbard, in a priceless bit of writing, put it this way:

> Try to fix firmly in your mind what you would like to do, and then without veering off direction, you will move straight to the goal. Keep your mind on the great and splendid things you would like to do, and then, as the days go gliding by, you will find yourself consciously seizing upon the opportunities that are required for the fulfillment of your desire. (This is subtle. If you think great things, you will unconsciously move toward them.)

Was Elbert Hubbard possibly guilty of overstating it a bit? We weren't sure, but the idea became deeply entrenched in our minds, and we began to understand a little better what Norman Vincent Peale meant when he said, "A mental concept has more voltage than electricity." And as we came to know Norman during the last ten years of his life, we often felt the voltage of his life and faith.

We feel the psychological idea here can be most helpful to any couple, whether they've been married one year, seven years, twenty years, or forty years: *When we truly believe that something will happen and vividly picture it happening, we subconsciously tend to act in a way that makes it happen.*

It is important not to confuse what we've been working through here with superficial pop psychology or some form of shallow positive thinking. We are talking about building positive, realistic dreams and goals.

The Excitement of Dreaming Together

While it is true that almost all marriages begin with unrealistic expectations, and dreams are dreamed that may be incapable of fulfillment in real-life marriage, we have come to feel through conversations with hundreds of people and through our own experiences that this need not spell doom to a relationship. But a marriage is likely to recover from weak or unrealistic expectations only as a couple *catches the excitement of dreaming together—continually, year after year, year in and year out.* For most of us this takes planned and calculated effort and constant practice. Possibly it may even seem a bit mechanical at first, but in time it will become a way of life.

Few humorists are more perceptive than Sam Levenson. His insights cut deep into the common experiences of life: "Love at first sight is easy to understand. It's when two people have been looking at each other for years that it becomes a miracle."[9] But it's a miracle born out of the dreams, hopes, and expectations of two people who refuse to let their marriage become humdrum and dull, with no more resiliency than wet and soggy cardboard.

Obviously, there are no pat answers, no heaven-sent formulas that insure success. But for us, dreams and affirmations shared on a regular basis—talked out and written down—have brought excitement and freshness to our marriage, especially during the last twenty-five years. We've done more new things and traveled to more new places than during all the earlier years. Not that it is easy. In fact, there are times when we're too angry and upset to dream or to expect better things tomorrow. But then, in time, our better sides take over, and we feel reassured of its value once again.

Building realistic expectations into the fabric of our lives, by focusing in on creative and mind-stretching affirmations and dreaming the sort of imaginative dreams that can add excitement and zest to the marriage relationship, is a risky and gutsy adventure. It is a rugged and tough exercise which takes nerve and work. But even in the midst of occasional failure we believe it's worth it.

Boyd is a trusted friend of ours, and a gifted communicator who I've always thought was just about too good to be true. He and Hazel have been married sixty-one years. In a recent conversation I asked him which year of his marriage had been the toughest. Much to my amazement he said, "Last year." Then I asked, "Which year was the best?" With a broad grin and a glint in his eyes, he responded immediately, "Next year will be."

Chapter Four

What Is Commitment?

> *Commitment is getting married and staying
> married because of the personal characteristics of
> the other person. I think there is a tendency to
> transcend problems when there is that bond that is
> basic for resolving them.*   Clifford H. Swensen

The whole concept of love is so distorted and per-
verted in our society that it is difficult for people to
get a clear sense of the proper basis for a marital
relationship. Our understanding of love is that it is
some kind of intoxicated frame of mind or a visitation
from outer space which overwhelms us and leaves a
person in an eternal state of being "high." As a family
counselor, I often see people who assume that since
they are no longer "high," they are no longer in love.
I usually tell my students here at Purdue that love is
a very poor basis on which to get married, and that if
all they have going for them is that they are in love,
then they need to terminate the relationship! I think
it takes a lot more than love on which to build a
marriage, . . . among these are loyalty, commitment,
money, etc.[1]

This portion of a letter from Dr. Wallace Denton of Purdue
University was more than a little shocking and puzzling
to Harriett and me. At the beginning of our marriage we
were on a "love high." While we understood the meaning

of loyalty, we were too immature to even begin to comprehend the meaning of commitment. And as for money, it just wasn't a problem—we didn't have any. But in 1938 everyone we knew was in the same boat, so we didn't feel sorry for ourselves. Further reflection, however, told us that because of the model our parents gave us, we had a heritage of commitment that would likely surface as the need arose.

Today, however, the idea and meaning of commitment in marriage is discussed with regularity in magazines ranging from *Women's Day* and *Cosmopolitan* to *Playboy*. And the daily newspaper often carries articles which attempt to explain the role and shape of commitment in today's changing world. Modern pundits of the marriage art solemnly declare that "commitment is the key to maintaining a sustained relationship." And, psychologist Joyce Brothers "feels that 'there is a very strong interest in commitment,' and that 'one of the top priorities in life for young people is a happy home and family life.' "[2]

There's a noble sound to such statements; but the feeling persists for us, possibly because of our Hoosier and Cornhusker roots, that the idea of "commitment" implies some kind of unpleasant teeth-gritting effort. Or, it could be that the almost unconscious negative reaction we have had to the word *commitment* is part of the residue from our somewhat authoritarian backgrounds. At any rate, whatever contributed to our earlier hang-ups, it wasn't until we had thoughtfully reexamined the meaning of commitment that we were able to get it out of a shadowy, lifeless, and somewhat negative state and into the flesh and blood realities of living.

Some Interpretations of Commitment

What does commitment mean? How far does it go? What is involved in commitment? How does it work in the raw edges of life? These are good but very hard questions—questions we've asked ourselves many times; questions we've asked couples married for twenty, thirty, forty years; questions we've asked people whose lives have been changed drastically by the trauma of divorce; questions we've asked competent persons involved in the helping professions.

Of course, the answers from these sources don't always come out the same. But, directly and indirectly, they have given us insights that form a sort of composite picture, deepening and bringing into focus a better understanding of what commitment can mean in a marriage relationship. Through these examples and a probing of our own feelings, we have certainly come to feel that love will inevitably have some soft spots. There is just no way that love in and of itself can be enough to bind two people together. Rather, we've come to believe that it is commitment that makes it possible to hold steady during times of severe distress and difficulty.

Scene 1—Bud and Elsie

The Carlsons were a proper couple, leaders in their community. Bud had inherited his father's business in a middle-sized upstate New York town. It wasn't a large business, but their home and manner reflected modest success. Both Bud and Elsie are leaders in their church; early in our conversation it came through clearly that this was an important part of their lives. It seemed at first that their responses were colored by surface proof-texts and pat phrases that had filtered their thinking and reactions for many years. But by the time we were ready to talk about commitment in their marriage, the conversation took on a greater depth. Their authentic commitment to each other and to their spiritual values was now very much apparent even in their lighter moments.

Bud, with a quick sideways glance at Elsie, said, "I heard somebody say one time that they had never considered divorce—murder, yes! That says it for me. Our marriage has been under attack from the day we started until now. If we were to list all of the things which might have broken it apart, we'd find, I am sure, that most of them are still present. But our commitment to each other and love for each other have held us together, and we've grown in the process. I wouldn't want it to be any different."

Scene 2—Roger and Eve

Roger Bates gave every appearance of being a shy, reserved man—a bit antiseptic. His lawyerlike responses to our questions were measured carefully. But still there was a softness about him which belied first impressions. As the oldest of three children in a home traumatized by divorce when he was sixteen, his eyes reflected the hurt he had felt as he remembered the violent conflict between his mother and father. His sense of shame and aloneness had scarred him deeply.

When Roger met and fell in love with Eve, it was a frightening experience for him. The very thought of marriage brought to the surface all of the insecurities and pain from his past. But with Eve's patient help and love, Roger worked through his feelings and they were married—and had been for twenty-seven years.

How did Roger rate commitment in their marriage relationship? "When I think of our marriage, the word *commitment* doesn't come to mind. Instead, the words which express my deepest feelings are *pure love*. Obviously, there's a certain amount of turmoil in any close relationship, and that is true with us. But on our marriage scale, love has always completely outweighed any turmoil. I suppose if the turmoil side of our scale ever reached the point to where it outbalanced the love side, we'd have to consider the commitment factor. But that has never happened to us—the love side has always been heavier.

"I don't think I am enslaved by my past any longer, but I suppose my thinking is still colored by it. In my opinion, so-called commitment kept a lot of older marriages intact that shouldn't have been held together. Commitment to something—I'm not sure what—held my mother and father together for at least five years longer than it should have. Those years were sheer hell for all of us. That, and the final divorce, almost ruined my thought of ever getting married, and it so scarred my two sisters that both of their marriage attempts have ended in failure—not once, but twice. And today they are so bitter that life doesn't have much meaning for either of them."

Scene 3—Varied Responses

Elwood, another person we questioned, disclosed similar feelings about commitment to those expressed by Bud: "Argue, yes, but divorce, never! I was determined that my marriage was going to work because my mother's and father's did not. So, come hell or high water, mine was going to work and that was it."

Willard, a precise and orderly accountant, approached this question from another angle: "Commitment to marriage itself or to each other? If you mean to each other, I can buy that. But if you mean just to marriage as something to be maintained, that would be more abstract, and I don't think I'd go along with that. I feel committed to people rather than to institutions."

Gen was still hurting from last year's divorce after twenty-one years of marriage: "At first I thought Al was committed to me and to our marriage. But it wasn't long before I began to feel that he was interested only in himself. He didn't seem to care about my needs and desires. As long as he was satisfied, even in our sex life, nothing else seemed to matter. And as long as we did what he wanted and went where he wanted to go, everything was all right. He never seemed interested in me as a person. I hung on over the years hoping it would change and scared to death that I couldn't make it alone. No, I guess I don't know anything about real commitment in marriage. I didn't even see it in my parents' marriage. My father was committed to just one thing—his job. Everything else took a back seat. Maybe someday yet I'll have my chance."

Olga expressed it this way: "We both enjoy the marriage relationship—the closeness, the warmth, and the commitment. I believe in the institution of marriage. I am committed to George as a person. I love him a lot more now than I did when I married him."

Satisfying Commitment

In an interview in 1977, Hubert Humphrey, at that time fighting his battle with cancer, said this about the lady he was married to for thirty-nine years:

> Muriel and I were saying the other day wouldn't it be terrible if we didn't really love each other because in a sense we're compelled to be together. I just can't imagine how miserable it would be if you had somebody you wish weren't near, and that happens to people, regrettably, in life. But she's been very tolerant of me and my ambitions, and now we have a kind of softness with each other, a tenderness that maybe we didn't have since we were youngsters first in love. Frankly, life is somewhat different for us because of my illness, and it's so good, so good just to have someone you can enjoy just reaching over and touching.[3]

Somehow, Hubert and Muriel Humphrey had discovered the meaning of commitment that was satisfying in their demanding relationship. Just a few days before this interview was taken he had been sworn in for his fifth term in the United States Senate, and sandwiched in between his terms of service in the Senate was a four-year stint as vice president of the United States. Throughout all of Senator Humphrey's tempestuous years of public life, he and Mrs. Humphrey mirrored a form of commitment with enduring quality. They indeed seemed to model a central theme of the 1979 National Assembly on the Future of the Family, sponsored by a coalition of women's movement organizations: "One basic premise of the assembly was to help our citizens preserve the one most essential element in all families—mutual support based upon a caring-and-sharing relationship."[4]

Commitment in Focus

We suspect that while most married couples would define and interpret commitment in varying terms, certain common threads seem to be woven into the fabric of lasting relationships by both persons. It is even possible that for many of us, to this point, the struggle for understanding has been more unconscious and intuitive than carefully thought through and expressed. Nevertheless, our life patterns tend to reveal an awareness of commitment as a life principle that suggests satisfaction and fulfillment.

In explaining their understanding of commitment, authors William Masters and Virginia Johnson help us to bring its meaning into focus:

A commitment is a pledge to do something. One person tells another, "I promise," and the promise is kept, the obligation fulfilled. Trust has been asked for; trust has been given, and trust has been repaid. This is the basic meaning of commitment. It is the cement that binds individuals and groups together. Without the ability of one person to rely on another, the social bond could not exist. . . . When the association is for emotional reasons, however, the meaning of commitment changes. It can still be defined as a pledge to do something, but the pledge possesses a radically different dimension. "I promise," one person tells the other, "because I care about you."[5]

The Root of Caring for Another

Commitment—promises kept; caring deeply about another person; the capacity to wholly love another person—*finds its roots in part, we believe, in our ability first to love and accept ourselves.* The biblical admonition suggests that we love others *as we love ourselves,* and this involves self-esteem, or self-acceptance, a living principle involved in every relationship, but especially marriage.

Somehow our ability to trust another person, to care deeply for another, grows out of an environment of self-trust and healthy self-love. Eric Hoffer, the colorful longshoreman philosopher, writes, "The remarkable thing is that we really love our neighbor as ourselves. We are tolerant toward others when we tolerate ourselves. We are prone to sacrifice others when we are ready to sacrifice ourselves. . . . It is not love of self but hatred of self which is at the root of the troubles that afflict our world."[6] And Rabbi Joshua Liebman endorsed Eric Hoffer's thinking in these words, "Love and believe in yourself properly and you will love and believe in your neighbor."

This is not to say that we won't have our flashes of self-doubt. There is much about our impersonalized culture that can cause us to feel we don't count, that we're not O.K., that we are mere cogs in a human machine or holes punched in a computer card. We all fight a continual battle against oblivion and protest forcefully against being taken for granted. But as we remind ourselves regularly that we are unique, that in the miracle of God's creation no two sets of fingerprints are alike, and that he has given us enormous capabilities, we come to accept ourselves as responsible persons. And in doing so, we grow to trust and accept others without feeling threatened and insecure. This, we believe, is the base for the pyramid of marriage.

False Slogans

Social pundits are good at fixing labels. The 1960s were the "if it feels good, do it" years. The 1970s gave birth to the "me" generation. And the 1980s and 1990s have been dubbed the "value free" years. These, of course, are generalities. However, these slogans do express a mindset that focuses on personal rights and "doing my own thing," and that stresses the importance of being assertive and getting our own way by whatever manipulative techniques that work.

Harriett and I are inclined to believe that there is a calloused selfishness in this "me first," "get-my-own-way-no-matter-what" view of life that plays havoc with all forms of relationships, including marriage. Yes, how we feel is important. Many of us have struggled valiantly to capture the art of feeling good about ourselves and cooperating with the rhythms of life. But maturity brings an awareness that there is more to life than what "I want" and what "I feel." This kind of lifestyle bears no resemblance to the healthy kind of self-acceptance and self-love that sets the stage to love and care and accept someone else.

Gerald, a veteran of twenty-eight years of what appeared to be a four-star marriage, expressed well the kind of caring and commitment that grows out of healthy self-regard: "There are a lot of different factors to commitment, but I think our mutual concern for each other would be about as good a definition as I could give. I'm concerned about Cynthia and everything she does, feels, and thinks. And I believe she is concerned about me. How we cultivated this is hard to say. But I guess we feel it because over the years we've shared common interests and have worked at our marriage and have grown together."

Commitment Exceeds Feeling

Our own experience underlines the idea that commitment within the marriage relationship transcends and goes beyond feeling; it is a decision, consciously made. It is a choice made by two people to love in the deepest meaning of the word. It is not merely an expression of love symbolized by saying "I do" before a minister or judge. Rather, it is an authentic love acted out on a daily basis toward one's spouse.

Father Chuck Gallagher lends authority to this idea: "Love does not just happen; it is created through decisions we make, the give and take day-to-day relationships and by reflection, listening, and knowing ourselves, our strengths and our weaknesses."[7]

With all of the fumbling and distorted ideas about life during the first seven years of our marriage, we not only had physical and emotional feelings of love, but we deliberately chose to be married and to stay married. Dr. Viktor Frankl makes an astute observation: "Everything can be taken from a man but one thing: the last of the human freedoms—to choose one's attitude in any given set of circumstances, to choose one's own way."[8] Our choice has carried us through some painful and stressful times. And it was *ours*. If just one of us had made it, we would very likely not have stayed together.

This same idea was echoed by Ruth and Steve Heller. Ruth, after a rather long litany of dissatisfaction, said, "But we still have the things that are important to me. There have been times when I felt like we wouldn't stay together no matter what. But there is no other person I would want to live with, and no matter how bad things have gotten, I've asked myself, 'What is it I really want?' And then I realize I've already got everything I want—it is just a matter of making it all work. I can't get away from that, so I guess we will go on living together as long as we live."

Throughout this monologue, Steve had been listening intently. When Ruth finished, he quietly underscored what she had said with these few words, "I think we both really do want the same thing; it is just that we have different ways of going about it."

There's another side to the commitment coin. Mary Dawson had been divorced four years when we talked. She told us about the night her husband, a physician, came home and asked, "What if you had a patient who told you he didn't love his wife anymore; what would you tell him?" Her reply was, "I would tell him to go back home and pretend he loved her and stick with it. I believe he can start to love her again."

Even as she responded to her husband's question that night, Mary recalled, she had a sick feeling in the pit of her stomach. Intuition told her that he was talking about himself, not a patient. At least the last half of their twenty years together had been shot through with disappointments, broken promises, and more than once by jealous rage that stopped just short of violent physical abuse. Twice their marriage had been shaken by traumatic career changes, and the birth of an unwanted fourth child had threatened to tear up their relationship by the roots.

But Mary's commitment to the marriage held her steady. She was determined to make it work: "I thought he was always honest with me as I was with him." But then he walked out, and one month after the divorce was final he married a woman ten years younger who had small children.

"And, you know," Mary added with a curious blend of bitterness and wishful thinking in her voice, "up until just last Christmas I fantasized his divorcing that other woman and coming home. I still felt our marriage could work, and I was committed to it. But now, after finally facing reality just a few months ago, I know it's all dead."

For whatever reason, Mary's commitment was not shared by her husband, and unless a husband and wife achieve a blending of their commitment to each other and their marriage, there is little or no chance of sustaining and building an adventurous relationship. Obviously we were in no position to fix blame for the breakup of Mary's marriage. Deep misunderstandings of any kind, including a fractured marriage, are not one-sided; there is seldom such a thing as an "innocent party."

But here was one of several classic examples which emphasized again that a mutual understanding, a commitment in marriage, calls for both the husband and wife to *will* the building of the relationship if it is to last. Dr. Paul Tournier says succinctly: "The first condition for mutual understanding is the desire for, the seeking after, and the willing of that understanding."[9]

Scene 4—Doris and Horace

It was a crisp October evening when I drove out to the north side of San Antonio to meet Doris and Horace Ayres. The black, star-studded sky, reaching as far as I could see in all directions, was a breathtaking panorama of beauty. While I didn't know it at the time, it was this moving and beautiful witness that God was in his heaven that prepared me in part for meeting two amazing and utterly delightful people.

Doris and Horace had then been married almost forty years. There was an aliveness about them that charged the atmosphere—especially when they talked about their two daughters and five grandchildren.

Why had Doris married Horace? After admitting that they probably hadn't married for the best of reasons, Doris added, "All my girlfriends were getting married, and it was just the thing to do. But I think I married Horace because he was cute and sweet and had nice manners and we had fun together. I didn't know what love was."

To brace himself for the wedding Horace had a drink or two before he went to the church. Doris admitted to being concerned about whether or not the minister would smell it, but she was unaware at the time that this was merely a hint of things to come.

After this start, Horace buried himself in his work, in hunting and fishing, and in drinking. And Doris settled down as best she knew how to make a home. Over the years, his work with an international oil service company kept Horace away from home for long stretches of time. While he was always home on holidays, these usually gave him an additional excuse to "celebrate."

As the years passed, Horace's drinking accelerated. There was always a bottle in his desk drawer at the office and another one in the car. He explained, "I wasn't the type of person that closed the office at five o'clock and stopped off at a bar before going home. I would come straight home every night and continue drinking while waiting for dinner. Then I'd eat a big meal and drink some more until I was drunk, and by then it was time to go to bed.

"Doris was more or less a fixture in our home, as were both of my children. I have always been tremendously dedicated to my company, and I had a very responsible job. But when you're drinking, you don't have the ability to look at things the way you should. Now I can see that Doris completely raised the girls; I had very little to do with them."

Such was the pattern of the Ayres' marriage for well over thirty years—held together by children and by a deep underlying feeling of commitment to their relationship. It is true, though, that over the years they experienced a mixture of good times with the bad. During the good times Doris was buoyed with feelings of hope and felt she could cope. But then during the bad times she was overwhelmed with despair and felt pressed down with the seeming hopelessness of the situation.

Finally, in desperation, Doris sought help for herself through Al-Anon. Here she confronted the truth that Horace was an alcoholic, that he was sick. At the same time she began to realize that alcoholism is a family disease. She, too, was sick, but in a different way. Out of this, Doris worked at change in her own life and attitudes. Earlier anger and hostility began to disappear.

Then, as Horace put it, "I didn't know what alcoholism was or even that I was sick, but I did know I had to slow down my drinking. Why, the last three or four weeks that I drank I couldn't even go to the office. I sat right there in that chair and drank, went to bed, got up, and drank some more. Finally, I knew I had to have help, and I hospitalized myself."

Four years of sobriety for Horace had passed from the moment of that decision to the evening of our visit. Now, both he and Doris are completely dedicated to Alcoholics Anonymous (AA) and Al-Anon. Either will drop whatever they are doing when a telephone call for help comes from an alcoholic, and they spend countless nights sharing their own experiences with AA and Al-Anon groups. Both

Horace and Doris were very open and natural about their strong Christian commitment and loyalty to one of the leading churches in their city.

How is it now? Horace confides, "She tells me she loves me several times a day, and I try to do the same."

And Doris adds, "I'm so glad we stayed together. We are now becoming more real and dear to each other every day—with just an occasional exception. We have love like a great many people never have. I'm not afraid now, and Horace does not have to run away from himself any more, or from life. We *like* each other. He's a nice person—good, kind, fair, honest, a great sense of humor. I love him now; I always did. It was what alcohol did to him that I hated."

As I left the warmth of the Ayres' home that night and looked up, the stars seemed to shine brighter than before. There was a warm glow inside of me. I was glad that somehow Doris and Horace Ayres had managed to stay together for those thirty-six years or I would never have gotten to know them. How they did it and why they did it, I'll never understand. But of one thing I was sure—they were glad to be together, and their love for each other at sixty-three was exuberant and fresh and contagious.

The Slow Maturing of Commitment

Our marriage biography reflects an intriguing commitment pattern which probably is not unique to our own experience. During our early years we were consumed by the physical, sexual side of our relationship—we were committed to it. For several reasons, some of them good and some not, we did not experience sexual intercourse before we were married. The physical and emotional strain was painfully intense, so all of our pent-up sexual drive sought explosive release with clockwork regularity during our twenties as we were struggling to find our way into the adult world. For us, the physical side of marriage was paramount as we elbowed our way through early adulthood.

Then as we moved into our thirties, the form of our commitment took on subtle changes—the implications seemed to deepen. An awareness of each other's personhood began to emerge. We moved on to know ourselves and each other on emotional, intellectual, and spiritual levels—to find ourselves as two independent persons. It was at this time that we began to discover one another as people, not just lovers.

It was during our thirties and the first half of our forties that our life together took on a rhythm, an ebb and flow, in which our immature egocentricity began to give way to a more mature caring for the feelings, thoughts, and ambitions of each other. Our commitment to each other, to growth, and to change as it colored and flavored our married life seemed to take on new shapes. The fact that we were two distinctly different people demanded a succession of fresh looks at the changing course of our love and commitment to each other. We had in fact reached the place in our marriage described so well by a writer whose name is unknown to us: "Marriage is the deep, deep peace of the double bed after the hurly-burly of the chaise lounge."

During much of this time we were still caught up excessively in the "making good" syndrome in marriage, family, and profession. We carried forward, consciously and unconsciously, the imagined and real limitations imposed by childhood feelings and experiences. Frequently, buried skeletons from the distant past—mistakes, feelings of inadequacy, fears—emerged to embarrass and confuse us, and our day-to-day living took on a more complicated form. But without pattern or blueprint, our commitment to each other and to our marriage relationship involved changes of attitude toward much of what we had held sacred. But like most people, we found making changes difficult and painful, and any new idea was toxic if there was a chance it might push us into the unknown or the uncertain.

Those were turbulent and irksome years. Our relationship teetered first toward the comfort and sameness of the past, then it would totter toward our underlying desire for change and growth and new forms to our commitment. At times the tensions created by this kind of push-pull exacted a frightful emotional toll. When we were high, new commitment expressions within marriage were an exhilarating challenge. When we were low, any form of change was scary, and the unknown was threatening. We were acting like the kind of people Huckleberry Finn was talking about when he said, "That is just the way with some people. They get down on a thing when they don't know nothing about it."[10]

But in our better moments we began to sense a character and quality of relationship and life beyond anything we had experienced, and this seemed to keep us on course—sometimes in spite of ourselves. We're happy to report that the physical expression of our love and early commitment, while probably not as frequent or intense as it was in our twenties and thirties, has deepened and matured also, exceeding both physically and emotionally anything we could have fantasized then. And now as we've moved into and beyond later adulthood, we find that our commitment to each other and to our marriage demands constant renewals as well as new and different expressions.

A Model of Commitment

A moving example of love and commitment between two persons can be seen in the marriage of John McCormack, for many years Speaker of the United States House of Representatives.

John McCormack never went anywhere without Harriet. If a President called him to the White House for a consultation in the afternoon, the Speaker would order his driver to detour to the Washington Hotel, so that he could have Mrs. McCormack's company on the ride to 1600 Pennsylvania Avenue. If he went to a reception, if he gave a speech to a high school group, if he attended a fund raiser, Harriet was either at his side or out in the limousine waiting for him. He sent polite regrets to out-of-town speaking requests, pleading pressing business. The pressing business was dinner with his wife. . .

"Always be sweethearts," he would advise young newlyweds who came to see him at the Capitol. "You're sweethearts before you're married. If a husband and wife would carry the sweetheart stage prior to marriage *into* marriage, they wouldn't have many difficulties and troubles, despite the fact that life, at its best, is a stony, steep, uphill journey. . . . Being sweethearts," he insisted, "is a state of mind."[11]

Continuing and Conscious Commitment

Emerging from all of our study and conversations over the past three or four years comes this overriding theme: *to last, the marriage relationship calls for conscious, overt acts of commitment to each other and to the whole idea of marriage by both husband and wife.* Further, this commitment cannot be a one-time affirmation ("I told her I loved her when we were married; why should I have to tell her every day?"). For buried within each of us is the deep psychological need for constant reassurance, to know where we stand with our partner in the relationship of marriage. It is the awareness that we are loved and accepted that builds our own sense of self-esteem and self-acceptance and makes it possible to give and express love in return.

William James, the great psychologist of the early years in the twentieth century, seemed to understand this need when he said, "One of the deepest drives of human nature is the desire to be appreciated." To be loved and affirmed gives life meaning and purpose. And Rollo May amplifies this idea further when he writes, "We define love as *a delight in the presence of the other person and an affirming of his value and development as much as one's own.*"[12] To confirm the value of one's husband or wife is to express love and commitment through words and actions that daily give the assurance and confidence all of us desperately need.

But this kind of commitment doesn't happen by accident or through haphazard or willy-nilly circumstances—it is planned for, worked for, fought for, by two determined people. Doctors Kinsey, Pomeroy, and Martin reaffirm this truth:

> A preliminary examination of six thousand marital histories in the present study, and of nearly three thousand divorce histories, suggests that there may be nothing more important in a marriage than a determination that it shall persist. With such a determination, individuals force themselves to adjust and to accept situations which would seem sufficient grounds for a break-up, if continuation of the marriage were not the prime objective.[13]

Commitment on Purpose

Frequently, commitment comes out of extremely painful experiences. Perhaps one of the more subtle hazards to growth and maturity in the middle of today's preoccupation with ease and comfort is our unfaltering effort to avoid anything painful. And yet in our better moments we know through personal experience, and through the witness of searching and thoughtful people of all times, that growth and maturity come as the result of weathering difficult and painful experiences.

Some people we know sit down once a year, review where they've been and where they are, and recommit all that they are to each other for the next twelve months. We've not done it just that way, but it sounds like a good idea. We agree that what works for one couple or for us may not work just the same way for someone else. We also agree that commitment to love, to respect each other as unique persons, to grow, to change, is essential to a lasting relationship between a married couple working out and through their years together.

Harriett and I have discovered that this kind of loving commitment is an act of the will, and it is a process that calls for constant renewal throughout every stage and age of life. Paul Tournier energizes this whole notion: "Marriage is not a state, but a movement—a boundless adventure."[14] In other words, our commitment at the beginning of marriage or a year ago or even yesterday is not a state in which we can relax, but a movement that demands renewal and updating every day if it is to be kept alive and adventurous.

Perhaps one of the most profound stories we've ever read best illustrates the feeling and the meaning of two people being committed to each other in marriage. It is the story of Ginger and Veronica Coffee, Irish immigrants to Canada. Ginger was a simple, glandular man with little formal education and even less sensitivity to the complex push and pull of human relationships. He and Veronica had a tempestuous and lusty marriage.

While the "Luck of the Irish" slogan might aptly apply to many of his countrymen, Ginger had a penchant for bad luck. Nearly always in the wrong place at the right time or the right place at the wrong time, he found himself one day the victim of Veronica's infatuation with his more successful close friend and almost lost her for good.

Slowly, carefully, though, Ginger and Veronica began to inch back toward each other—neither seemed able to ignore their many years together—and finally, they decided to give it another try. In a reflective mood Ginger says to himself, "Don't you know that love isn't just going to bed? Love isn't an act, it's a whole life. It's staying with her now because she needs you; it's knowing you and she will still care about each other when sex and daydreams, fights, and futures—when all that's on the shelf and done with. I'll tell you what love is—it's you at seventy-five and her at seventy-one, each of you listening for the other's step in the next room, each afraid that a sudden silence, a sudden cry, could mean a lifetime's talk is over."[15]

Chapter Five

Making Sure You Understand Each Other

Communication is perhaps the most important of all topics in psychology. It is largely through communication that we become what we are; it is through communication that we learn what we know; it is largely through destructive communication that problems in human relationships are created, and it is through constructive communication that such problems are presented or solved.   Sven Wahlroos

Scene 1—Lydia and Linn

Lydia was an outgoing, attractive young woman in her late twenties. She radiated an aura of self-confidence and assurance. And her appearance matched her demeanor, combining into a portrait of Junior League style and class. But Linn, her husband of six years, seemed to come from a different mold.

In spite of Linn's athletic build and chiseled good looks, he seemed to suffer from a severe case of tongue-tied-itis when the conversation took on any but a superficial tone. He managed routine responses to small talk, but any attempts at conversation on a deeper level produced little more than awkward silences. And he evidently only talked with Lydia on a surface level and didn't listen or appear interested in what she had to say.

To escape a boring routine and a dull husband Lydia enrolled in night school, and it wasn't long before it became obvious that the teacher, a rather handsome man in his mid-forties, was attracted to her. One evening he asked her to remain after class and have coffee with him. And three weeks later they ended up together in a motel room.

Lydia described her feelings this way, "I didn't plan to go to a motel and get involved with him sexually. While it was O.K., I didn't particularly enjoy it. What I really wanted was communication, and he listened to me."

A Universal Need

This lonely woman was so starved for attention, in spite of her status in the community, that she was grateful to find a man who would talk to her on a feeling level and then would listen to what she was thinking and feeling. It was obvious that they communicated verbally as well as sexually. But it wasn't really sex she was starved for; rather it was someone to talk to and who cared enough for her to listen.

A conversation we had one warm, spring afternoon with Dr. Phyllis Hart, a Pasadena, California, psychologist, validated what we've heard from a couple of hundred people we've talked to: "A universal problem in troubled marriages, and in most marriages, is poor communication." Dr. Hart's reactions seem to relate to the kind of statistical data currently receiving attention: "The average couple married ten years or more spends only thirty-seven minutes a week in close communication."[1] Another authority varies the time slightly: "The average American couple spends twenty-six minutes a week in serious conversation."[2]

Dr. Joyce Brothers, in quoting a study done by the Family Service Association, reports that 87 percent of the persons interviewed said that communication was a major conflict in their marriages. And to compound the dismal reports, family sociologist Jessie Bernard believes that openness of communication is virtually nonexistent by middle age. "Conversation, 'just plain talk' between husband and wife never happens. . . . People become habituated to one another, but this is a far cry from companionship."[3]

The statistics vary, but the fact remains that out of 10,080 minutes a week, the above percentages don't add up favorably for most of us. Yet, we believe that *close communication, serious conversation, is at the very heart of a healthy marriage relationship.* A lack of close communication results in a hell on earth for two people, who day by day stumble into deeper areas of misunderstanding, frustration, and hurt until an explosion drives them apart or forces a confrontation which moves them toward solutions.

At other times, an absence of meaningful communication introduces a sterile accommodation process whereby, for whatever reason, a couple hangs together while each partner goes through the motions of doing his or her own thing with teeth-gritting determination to keep up appearances. Father Chuck Gallagher recognizes the deadliness of this lifestyle: "The tragedy of the normal marriage is not the horror of divorce or separation, or the major marital sins of adultery and cruelty, but the willingness to settle down into a comfortable pattern of getting along with one another at a high level of accommodation."[4] Even though such couples may give the appearance of success and are frequently in the mainstream of Middletown, U.S.A. society, their facade is phony. They know it; everybody knows it. But they keep on living the lie, perpetuating emotionally crippling damage to themselves and to their children.

Statistics don't bleed or breathe—but people do. So, first off, what about us? Has our marriage held together because we have become experts in the communication department? Heavens no! Deep in our backgrounds is the devastating "children are seen and not heard" syndrome. Both of us carried massive insecurities into marriage. And neither of us knew how to cope with even the barest expression of our feelings, although Harriett was far more outgoing and open than I.

Our backgrounds and the demands of society as we understood them locked us into the "bigger is better" notion. We were caught up in the lunacy that *doing* and *achieving* were more important than *being*. The doer, the striver for success, the person who clawed his or her way feverishly up the achievement ladder—these were held up as models to emulate. We thought this was the good life because that's what we understood it was all about. And so we held together, working at doing the right things. Our communication on a feeling level was sketchy and little more than superficial—except when Harriett forced me into the open through confrontation. We pretty well exemplified the observation of Alexis de Tocqueville, the nineteenth-century French writer, when he concluded that Americans could talk about everything but could not converse about anything.

There Must Be a Better Way

This was the pattern through most of the first twenty-five years of our marriage. But slowly we both began to experience the haunting feeling that there should be more, and that there could be a better way to communicate. And so our pilgrimage began to take on new shapes. For us, among the most life-changing new steps in our marriage was the one described here by Harriett: "One of the most important of these new shapes in our life together was the discovery that it was all right for me to verbalize my angry and hurt feelings. It seems strange now to think back on that time in my life when I believed my angry feelings should be pushed down out of sight, and that it was wrong to get them out in the open. But the marriage setting in which I grew up was outwardly very placid. At no time did my parents let any stress or tension between them be seen or felt by my brother and me. So I didn't even know how to go about expressing my anger in the right way; and besides, every time I did get angry, the feelings of guilt were intense. In my background it just wasn't an acceptable thing to do.

"But as Floyd and I worked through these phony feelings of guilt, which we both shared to a degree, we came to understand that it was good for us to get our feelings out on top of the table. We realized that repressed anger and hurt can make us sick emotionally and physically, and usually erupts in a more dangerous way if it is held in very long. Believe me, the discovery of this new shape to our relationship was very freeing to me. It was a great release to know that it was all right for me to express my feelings, even though it might push us into a precarious or fragile scene—and sometimes it does!"

Slowly we came to see that life was meant to be fun. And as we began to learn the art of sharing our thoughts and feelings on a deeper level, our lives seemed to open up. We discovered an excitement and a richness that exceeded anything we could have dreamed of.

We still have our outbursts of juvenility, with disagreements and, occasionally, a good scrap. More often than not, neither of us starts off handling these conflicts very well. And now and then I fall into the old trap of retreating into a silent shell with feelings of self-serving outrage. But it happens less often than it used to, and as time passes I seem to bounce back faster. We are living examples of the idea that communication "is not a goal that you will ultimately reach or an achievement of some kind. It's a process—the circulatory system of marriage."[5]

Seeing Through Different Lenses

Slowly, Harriett and I are beginning to understand how our efforts to communicate get fouled up because both our methods of sending and receiving are so affected and influenced by our backgrounds and culture. Each of us has been "taught to 'see' what we see and to 'hear' what we hear."[6] This process began in the earliest days of our infancy as we were influenced by our parents' attitudes and perceptions of life. Their moral, religious, economic, and philosophical concepts became ours, either to follow or react against.

In addition, we were influenced by the broader social contexts in which we grew up. Somerset Maugham summed up this idea in a general way:

> For men and women are not only themselves; they are also the region in which they were born, the city apartment or farm in which they learned to walk, the games they played as children, the old wives' tales they overheard, the schools they attended, the sports they followed, the poets they read, and the God they believed in.[7]

Don Fabun, whose writing put expression to some thoughts of ours that were beginning to emerge, says:

> A very cogent argument could be developed that there are $3\frac{1}{2}$ billion different languages in the world. Each of us talks, listens, and thinks in his own special language (and sometimes he uses several) which contains slight variations of agreed-upon meanings that are uniquely individual, and which may change each second. Our personal language is shaped by our culture, country, province, section, neighborhood,

profession, personality, attitudes, and mood of the moment. And the chances that even a few of us will share all of these 'ingredients' in the same way at the same time is pretty remote.[8]

Where we grew up in various parts of California, our schooling, the kinds of people we knew, where we vacationed, the church we attended, the books we read, the people we dated—all of these gave us uniquely different experiences. When we married, we tried to bring together these two widely divergent sets of understanding of what we "saw" and "heard." And we frequently failed to understand each other.

It is true for Harriett and me that over the past fifty years there has been a gradual blending of many of our perceptions; we may see and hear more things alike than we once did. Nevertheless, as two distinctly different persons, we still see, hear, and interpret things, consciously and unconsciously, through the lenses and filters of all that has gone into making us who and what we are.

We have laughed and argued for years over little ways that we see and interpret things differently: If we have to drive two cars to the same place, we always go by two different routes, with each of us convinced our particular way is best; we never tackle a mathematical problem from the same starting point; and when I refer to the "outside lane" of a highway, Harriett sees it as the "inside lane."

Hindsight, of course, is always a marvelous instrument in revealing what might have been. It's clear now that we cannot assume we see or hear something in just the same way our partner does. But if we, somehow, could have come earlier to the beginnings of an understanding and celebrating of our differences, many hurtful confrontations could have been avoided. There's a profound truth here which, when grasped and worked with at any age, can revolutionize communication within the marriage relationship.

What Is Communication?

Psychologist Clifford Swensen of Purdue University states that most couples who have been married a long time grow less affectionate toward each other with the passing years. He surveyed five hundred couples who had been married for at least twenty years, and they generally agreed that verbal expressions of love diminished with the passing of time.[9] We believe that a lack of deep and intimate communication is responsible in large measure for this frightening trend.

But, unfortunately, the word *communication* has been thrown around so much lately that it has become a cliché. In our scramble for understanding we've just had to break it down into simple forms, trying to get it out of the realm of clichés and onto a feeling level. Only when this happens can two people who've said "I do" begin to grasp the meaning of open and deep sharing, and of how to begin making it work with a potential for a lasting relationship.

Put simply, *communication involves what we say, how we say it, how we receive what is said, and what we don't say.* It involves a thoughtful look at how and on what level a couple express their thoughts and feelings to each other. Effective communication, according to one authority, depends almost entirely on the attitude of the sender toward the receiver.[10] In other words, if the sender is uptight or angry or fearful, it is almost certain that identical emotions will be aroused in the receiver; or, if the sender radiates satisfaction, love, or bubbly joy, these same feelings will likely be picked up and sent back by the receiver.

There's a sobering principle here which calls for a close look. Except for unusual circumstances, *we usually receive in the same spirit we have given.* If our verbal signals in a conversation are accusatory or critical, defenses will be thrown up and response will usually reflect the sender's attitudes. On the other hand, warm messages of love and understanding and acceptance will usually evoke a like response.

Scene 2—Iris

When we first met and talked with Iris in her well-kept suburban home, she had been divorced two years—the curtain had fallen on twenty-one years of marriage. Obviously, the reasons that cause any long-term marriage to crumble are complex and never one-sided. However, it soon became apparent that Iris and Fritz had meandered through twenty-one years of playing house without anything more than a cursory stab at deep and meaningful communication. They didn't fight or argue over even the normal, daily irritations that plague every relationship. Negative feelings were bottled up, as well as expressions of positive feelings. Their relationship suffered from the blahs.

Then one day Fritz announced that he was leaving, and for good. But a few minutes later, in the sudden and unexpected heat of the scene that followed his "I'm moving out" speech, he petulantly announced his willingness to stay if Carol, their sixteen-year old daughter, would stop leaving her stuff scattered around the family room, and if Bud would mow the lawn and carry out the trash without being told to all the time. "If you will all shape up, I'll stay."

Twenty-one years of marriage in the background and still the masks couldn't come off and gut level issues be discussed. For them it was too late, and they became one more statistic in the divorce epidemic sweeping through our society today.

Scene 3—Glenn

Glenn and I had been talking for a couple of hours in his law office on the twenty-third floor. The sun had disappeared into the Pacific Ocean a half hour or so before, and now the lights were beginning to blink on across the sprawling city of Los Angeles. We'd talked about his twenty-four years of marriage to Elsie that had collapsed nine months before.

Early in our conversation the words tumbled out in the rather precise fashion characteristic of attorneys. But now Glenn's sentences were punctuated with long periods of reflective silence. He recalled some good early years, but then he and Elsie had slowly begun to grow apart. Resentment and anger replaced early acceptance and love. "A lot of things just didn't get said. One of Elsie's complaints was that I never would argue. She liked to talk things out, but when we got off into that, my below-the-surface anger and resentment crystalized. After those scenes, everything was straightened out as far as she was concerned, but I was all tied up in knots inside and it would take me several days to work through my feelings. She seemed to get closure when we talked things out, but I never did. We were always talking at different levels, so we never came out at the same place and I just retreated more and more into silence."

As I was about to leave, Glenn said, "I think the kind of advice I would give to people setting out on a long-term relationship would be to start with how crucial adequate communication is. And I'm talking about the communication of feelings on a gut level. Elsie and I talked, but not about the important things."

Was Elsie the sole cause of the communication breakdown which ultimately wrecked this relationship? We doubt it. No postmortem can fix blame. We had just his side of the story at the time, but one thing seemed to come through: somewhere along the line Glenn and Elsie lost their sensitive awareness of each other and stopped trying.

Hints for Meaningful Communication

We believe that growth in communication in marriage is the result of conscious decisions deliberately made. Probably none of us begin to move out of the closedness of our particular shells and toward openness with each other without confronting a crisis and exerting enormous effort. This has certainly been true in our own marriage. But an awareness of several key ingredients we've culled from our research can help any couple's communication become more meaningful.

1. *It's what you say that counts.* We agree with the observation that clear communication is far more than just an exchange of words; it is a meeting of minds.[11] Yet, there's no question that we've come to value the importance of words themselves. Whether a couple has been married twenty-four hours or forty-one years, there's magic in the words "I love you," provided that tone of voice and day-to-day actions validate and deepen the meaning of the words. We all need desperately to hear and feel that we're cared for, that we're O.K., that our weaknesses are understood and our strengths are appreciated.

That all sounds simple and sensible, but somehow most of us get so fouled up with the mechanics of making our way up the social, business, and professional ladders, that we frequently fail to extend to our husband or wife the same polite and thoughtful courtesies we easily extend to a friend or business associate. The people we are closest to often never hear how we appreciate them. Dr. Cecil Osborne, a good friend of ours and a highly competent therapist, offers this quote from an unknown source: "If we knew the world was going to end in five minutes, every phone booth would be jammed with people trying to stammer out to someone, 'I love you.' "

Little by little we've come to understand, when we're at our best, that it is just as easy, if we set our minds to it, to be complimentary and affirmative of each other as it is to be negative and picky. And it's a lot more fun. There's no doubt that at first it may take a lot of conscious effort, if being positive and affirmative has not been a way of life. In other words, we'll have to work at it, but in time this can become a habit, even as being critical and cutting is a habit.

There's an important aspect of this area of communication that we've just begun to work through: Be explicit in your praise. A broadly generalized affirmation statement doesn't really cost the sender much, and it says little to the intended receiver. For example, "Helen, you always fix good dinners" or "Jim, you look nice tonight." How much more it means to be specific and say:

"That was a great dinner tonight. I liked the dressing you had on the fruit salad."

"Darling, I love *you*."

"You really look trim and streamlined in your new camel's hair jacket when you wear it with those gray slacks."

"Wow, you sure turn me on when you wear that new, black party dress. It accentuates the positive in all the right places."

No matter how self-assured we are most of the time—no matter how much we may seem to have it all together—we all need the positive affirmation of our spouse.

2. *Words have power.* A few years ago as we attempted to share our feelings and to understand one another better, we became acutely conscious of the importance of the

words we use, and that words produce emotion. They are capable of inflicting deep hurt, feelings of inferiority, strong stirrings of anger and hostility, feelings of defensiveness and burning hate, or a haunting sense of aloneness and isolation. At the same time, words can boost our self-esteem by giving us warm feelings of being loved and appreciated—the exquisite awareness of sexual stimulation, the excitement of wanting and being wanted, the joy of feeling that we're number one with our mate.

And frequently, the use of the right words can creatively avert hostility and misunderstanding in moments of crisis. For example, during the 1962 Cuban crisis when Russia and the United States of America confronted each other because of the presence of missiles in Cuba, the world hovered breathlessly for several days on the verge of possible nuclear disaster. Instead of a blockade, President Kennedy imposed a *quarantine* on Cuba. A blockade would have been an act of war, but nobody knew just what the implications were to a *quarantine*. The use of that word gave a clear signal that we intended to protect ourselves, but it also indicated that we wanted, if at all possible, to avoid war. Using an intentionally vague word was part of our strategy. And it was this careful and thoughtful choice of words which forestalled shooting until tempers cooled and reason could prevail.

3. *It's important to be specific.* At the same time, being specific is of equal importance if we are to maintain clear communication and prevent negative feelings which can lead to a breakdown. We learned our lesson about this the hard way several years ago on a cold night just before Christmas. Harriett and I had been shopping together on Hollywood Boulevard, but then we agreed to separate for a time and meet at eight o'clock at the front entrance of the

Broadway Department Store at the corner of Hollywood and Vine.

I arrived right on time and took up my position just outside the revolving door. I waited five minutes, fifteen minutes, thirty minutes. By this time I was chilled to the bone from the cold wind, but hot under the collar from self-righteous anger. *What was wrong? We said we'd meet right outside the door at eight o'clock; how could Harriett be so thoughtless as to leave me here in the cold while she was probably puttering around some sale table in a warm store?* The longer I stood there the madder I got and colder I felt.

Finally, at nine o'clock I was so cold I just couldn't take it any longer, and I whirled through that revolving door and there stood Harriett on the inside. Boy, was she mad! "Where have you been? We agreed we'd meet *inside* the revolving door at eight o'clock, and I've been right here all the time."

We rode home that night in stony silence, each of us convinced the other was wrong. But after an hour or so the funny side to the whole thing began to filter through. There we were, not over twelve feet apart for a solid hour—Harriett on the inside of the door, I on the outside, because of indefinite and fuzzy communication. And to this day when we agree to meet, recollection of that scene insures clear communication.

4. *Avoid buzz words and phrases.* We've realized that certain words and phrases are usually sure to be inflammatory and release jangling, negative feelings of resentment or defensiveness. Such words as *always* and *never,* when used with the wrong combination, are almost certain to run up red flags:

"You *always* interrupt me when I'm telling a story."

"You are *never* pleasant to my mother when she visits us."

"You *always* work late when I want to go out."

"You're *never* ready to go when I am."

Whether sugar-coated or dipped in acid, there's no way anything good can come out of a choice of words that obviously points an accusing finger at the other person's weakness. Blame or attack words are emotionally crippling and destructive. What's worse, they become a habit and can so easily build discontent upon discontent until a marriage is destroyed.

Closely related to the *always* and *never* buzz words are what Robert Ball calls "God Almighty" statements. With such statements, "it's like the heavens open, and these words drop down from on high as if spoken by God himself. . . . They leave no room for exception or reservation. They give the impression that 'that's the way it is!'"[12] Some examples he gives of "God Almighty" statements include:

"Nobody understands me!"

"You never get home on time!"

"You don't care one thing about me or the kids!"

"You never listen to me!"

"Things just aren't like they used to be!"

"Nobody cares about doing good work any more!"

Reading these vast, sweeping accusations reminded me of some of the statements Harriett and I throw around at times: "You always interrupt me when I'm trying to make a point!" "I never get to finish a sentence!" "I'm never able to measure up to what you expect!" "You always take your briefcase on our vacations!" When you stop to think about it, there's just no good comeback to a "God Almighty" statement. No wonder they make us mad and completely foul up communication between a husband and wife or between parents and children.

What's the answer? How do you defuse this communication stopper? Bob Ball suggests using "I feel" statements instead of "God Almighty" statements:

"I feel left out when you don't include me in the conversation."

"I feel neglected when you don't call and tell me you will be late getting home."

"I feel unimportant to you when you work so much of the time."

"I feel that watching television is more interesting to you than talking with me."

These are helpful because there's nothing accusatory about an "I feel" statement. You're not making a judgment of the other person; you're simply saying how you feel, and there's a big difference. For Harriett and me, the "I feel" formula is invaluable in learning to say what we really mean. My dogmatic generalizations are beginning to occur less frequently, and when one of us slips, all the other has to say to defuse the explosive potential is, "Boy, that sure was a 'God Almighty' statement." Then the scene usually ends with a laugh instead of an argument.

5. *Put-downs aren't funny.* It was a bitterly cold, five-below-zero afternoon when we interviewed Helen and Vic in their stately, everything-in-its-place home. Oak logs burned evenly in their spacious, antique brick fireplace, but they couldn't dispel the cold atmosphere that seemed to penetrate every corner of the wood-paneled family room. At one point Helen blurted, "When I get to feeling critical of Vic, I use plain, straight-to-the-point words."

To which Vic responded through pursed lips, "To put it bluntly, she gets mad and nothing is left to my imagination. She always gives it to me straight out." It wasn't clear what held them together in this luxuriously appointed armed camp, but it was obvious their attempts at communication had long ago deteriorated to a negative litany of carping criticism, relieved now and then by less angry but razor-sharp put-downs.

Very much like this dangerous and emotionally treacherous game of words is the poorly disguised "joking" put-down. It's amazingly easy to slide into this snide approach of venting dissatisfaction and hostility toward one's husband or wife: "Vera's still got a good figure. There's just more of it than there used to be, but *most* of it is still in the right places." Both the words and tone of voice underline the fact that Vera's weight is a bone of contention in their home, and probably not the only one at that. The jesting remark, loaded with innuendo, is without doubt one of the cruelest and most devastating and unfunny bits of verbal disaster to rock any marriage.

6. *It's how you say it.* Frequently, it's not *what* we say, but the *way* we say it that disrupts the communication process in the best of marriages. A tone we use or a different style of conversing can often be misunderstood and be destructive. We have a couple of young friends, from dramatically different backgrounds, who fortunately came to terms early with this fact.

Leone is Italian—an olive-skinned beauty with long black hair, dancing dark eyes, a bubbly, outgoing manner. Everything she does becomes a major production, a dramatic event, with voice and gestures in fortissimo. In her home they never just talked, they yelled. It was as natural a means of communication in their way of life as eating lasagne every Saturday night. During their engagement Lee kept telling her he just couldn't live that way. She needed to learn to talk quietly so they could understand each other. But Leone could take this just so long and then she'd say, "I'm getting so tired of talking. In our family we yell at each other."

Happily, Leone and Lee developed a caring sensitivity to their conflicting styles and backgrounds. Each worked at trying to understand the reactions of the other, and thus often avoided potential misunderstandings.

7. *Timing can be everything.* Effective communication between any two persons—especially a wife and husband—seems possible only when thoughtful attention is given to timing. I usually pop out of bed at least by five in the morning, and I'm alert and sharp until evening; then it's downhill all the way. On the other hand, Harriett struggles reluctantly out of bed as late as possible, and we say very little until after her first cup of coffee. Then she keeps pumping herself up the rest of the day, until by evening she's in high gear. In other words, she is a night person; I'm a morning person.

Now, we have known this for most of our married life. But for some reason we were blind for a few years to just how important this difference was to our success or failure in communicating with each other. We had some noisy misunderstandings and hurt feelings because I was all psyched up to discuss plans for our Christmas vacation at seven o'clock in the morning, while Harriett would have preferred to hold that discussion at ten-thirty at night.

Slowly but surely we've come to understand and respect our differences. We have learned to time our serious discussions so as to avoid each other's low periods.

One friend of ours usually times her serious discussions with her husband after she's fed him his favorite dinner. We've learned to schedule our sharing and times of deep discussion with our own particular version of a late afternoon "happy hour"—a period when our metabolism seems to hover on an almost equal level. And so, for an hour or two this is our time for serious conversation, discussing plans or dreams, the airing of differences, sharing the events of the day, or just plain visiting. It makes for a late dinner, but we have come to like that ritual too. This is now a time each of us looks forward to.

Obviously, our timing won't work for everybody. But the point is, every couple can develop a sensitivity to good communication timing and avoid many of those heated, emotional moments in which harsh words are exchanged that evoke feelings of hurt and anger. It takes planning and effort, but the rewards are worth it as potentially inflammatory discussions are deferred by thoughtful timing.

8. Listening is an art. Of primary importance to good communication is two-way interaction—sending and receiving, speaking and listening. Most of us spend so much of our time broadcasting that we have little opportunity left to receive.

Occasionally Harriett will say, "You're hearing me, but you aren't listening to me." And she's right, or I wouldn't interrupt her in midsentence with my own version of what I think she's going to say, only to discover that I was not only rude when I did that, but wrong.

We agree with Paul Tillich when he said, "The first duty of love is to listen." Masters and Johnson confirm this truth: "They [husbands and wives] must learn to communicate, not simply with words, but also with touch or a glance that needs no explanation. Above all, a man and woman must learn to be present with each other—not just to look, but see; not just to hear, but to listen; not just to talk, but to commune."[13]

Hearing is passive; listening is active. Listening demands concentration: thinking with the other person; attempting to become involved not only with words but with the feelings of the other person; listening to what is being said as well as to what isn't being said. In fact, listening is hard work. It requires energy and concentration and involvement with the other person.

For us, listening is a meeting of the eyes, the windows of the soul. It is the response of caring. It tries hard to understand at all cost. Psychologist Sven Wahlroos wraps up this idea neatly: "The first thing we must keep in mind about listening is that it must be *active* if it is to be effective. Active listening implies an obvious interest in the partner's feelings and opinions as well as an active effort to hear and understand the partner."[14]

But there's a tricky factor to our act of listening to each other, and that is the realization that we listen out of our own environment and through our own perceptions at any given moment. If I have had a hairy day at the office and feel misunderstood and not appreciated, it affects not only the content and sound of *my* words, but it also influences what I am able to *hear*. In a sense, my listening filters are clogged with the day's debris, and unless I'm consciously aware of this, any attempt at closeness and openness in conversation may be sabotaged. In fact, we've come to understand a little better the idea that what we hear and the way we hear it is deeply colored by our past conditioning and experiences.

This comment from Dr. Paul Tournier is one that I read and reread regularly because I know what he says is true, but I find it so easy to become careless and forget: "It is impossible to overemphasize the immense need humans have to be really listened to, to be taken seriously, to be understood. No one can develop freely in this world and find life without feeling understood by at least one person."[15] We believe that listening is *the* way to understanding and growth and healthy communication within the marriage relationship. Or, as Reuel Howe has said, "Listening is a key to *knowing* and *understanding*."

9. Don't just say it—write it. Gwen Statler thought back to a few years ago when, after reading a book on marriage, she sat down and wrote out a long list of things that she liked about her husband, Will. It took Gwen all afternoon to do this, because once she got started it became sort of a game to think back year after year over each of the twenty-three years of their life together. And the more she thought about it, the longer the list got. Finally, just moments before Will was due home from the office, she finished, reread the list for the last time, and then stashed it away in the privacy of one of her desk drawers.

Then, just a year before our conversation with the Statlers, the leader of one of their Sunday school class sessions suggested that the husbands and wives each write a letter in which they enumerate all of the things they like about each other. So Will sat down and wrote Gwen a long letter in which he spelled out in considerable detail all the things he liked about her. At dinner a night or so later he handed her the letter. As soon as Gwen saw what it was, she excused herself, slipped back to her desk, reached way back into the bottom drawer, pulled out the four-year-old paper, and handed it to her husband.

Will said to us, "You know, when I read that list and realized that she had written it four years ago, I couldn't help but cry a little. It made me feel really good, and I carry it around in my briefcase all the time."

How about that? What a great idea! In fact, this is one of the helpful techniques that counselors and Marriage Encounter sessions have employed for years—to have a husband and wife write out their deepest feelings about each other, and then share what they've written.

We've not done that in quite the same way as Will and Glen Statler did. But as writers we both readily agree that sometimes when we have thoughtfully expressed our deep feelings about each other on cards at Christmas, Valentine's Day, birthdays, Mother's Day or Father's Day, wedding anniversaries, or other special days, it has been a moving and deeply meaningful experience. Each of us has drawers piled high with such cards.

We certainly identify with what Father Gallagher says:

> The spoken word is . . . an absolutely essential form of communication between spouses. But it has definite disadvantages. Husbands and wives—particularly those in good marriages who have talked together a lot—tend after a number of years to believe they know what the other person if going to say. They often finish the other's sentence, at least interiorly, and don't really listen to all that is actually being said.[16]

People we've talked to who have tried any variation of written dialogue attest enthusiastically to its effectiveness in marriage communication. In most cases, when we have settled down to write about our thoughts and feelings, much more consideration is given to the ideas we want to express and to our selection of words than when we speak. Most of us do better when we have taken the time to think things through.

10. Meaningful dialogue pays off. This begins to probe at a profound level into the whole idea of communication between husband and wife. It is in the deep sharing of feelings that we come to know each other. Reuel Howe observed, "Only as we know another and are known by him, can we know ourselves."[17] The Swiss psychiatrist Paul Tournier echoes this truth: "To fail to understand one's spouse is to fail to understand oneself. It is also a failure to grow and to fulfill one's possibilities."[18]

It is in sharing, in dialogue—verbal or written—that meaning flows back and forth between two persons. Here the masks are off, the defenses are down—mutual love and understanding make them unnecessary—and we become vulnerable to each other. An awareness of the needs, hurts, ambitions, and goals of each other becomes a powerful force that can move us toward understanding and an ever deeper relationship.

The priority and the meaning of dialogue are summed up incomparably by Reuel Howe: "Dialogue is to love what blood is to the body. When the flow of blood stops, the body dies. When dialogue stops, love dies and resentment and hate are born. But dialogue can restore a dead relationship into being, and it can bring into being once again a relationship that has died."[19]

Perhaps the most important of all attempts at the verbal communication of thoughts and feelings and ideas should take place within the marriage and family relationship. And yet, it is in this arena that most of us find ourselves the least prepared. But in our conversations with the many people we've interviewed, and through our own experience, faulty though it may be, we've concluded that one major key to a happy and rewarding long-term marriage comes through a consistent effort at the level of deep dialogue Reuel Howe describes. And the good news is that it works when two people are committed to making it happen.

Communicating as Equal Partners

Harriett and I believe strongly in equalitarian or equal partner marriage. Neither of us can say that we brought this idea into the beginnings of our relationship. But we do know that it has been uppermost in our thinking for the last twenty-five years as we have struggled in our efforts to communicate with each other in a mutually satisfactory way.

We feel it is important to take a brief look at this concept of marriage in connection with a comfortable and effective pattern of verbal communication between a husband and wife. Somehow we have the feeling that clear lines of open communication are only likely to be possible between persons of equal status in any relationship. For example, we question the possibility of clear, open, and honest lines of communication between any two adults if one of them has veto power over the other. It is a rare instance in which communication channels are completely open between employer and employee. After all, human nature being what it is, with the drive for self-preservation always in our minds, there is a point beyond which a person cannot go if the other party asserts headship, abandons negotiation, and arbitrarily imposes a decision. The person who can be overruled is always at a disadvantage, and, for us at least, this makes it virtually impossible to maintain open lines of communication.

It is not our purpose in this brief section to become embroiled in the traditional arguments on hierarchical views of marriage as opposed to equal partnership. Rather, we lean on our personal experience, and this view was shared by a significant number of the persons we interviewed. We recognize the belief that an organization cannot function effectively under two heads. However, we cannot accept the idea that this principle applies to a relationship as sensitive and delicate as marriage.

Over these past years Harriett and I have shared jointly in our decisions. If we could not agree, we didn't act, but we kept talking—the communication line remained open. At times we've reached a common opinion; other times we haven't. But neither of us believes that our judgment is infallible. Now and then we are sure we were both wrong, but we would rather risk that than impair our relationship by imposing our will on the other. This ingredient has been vital to the success of our long-term marriage, even though we readily admit to some tense and angry moments in the process.

Open and honest verbal communication is indeed essential to the marriage relationship—by two people who care deeply for and are sensitive to the needs and concerns and feelings of each other. How we say it with words is the key to a fulfilling and enriching life together.

Chapter Six

Communicating without Words

The ability to communicate in mutually affirming ways is the fundamental skill which is essential to the growth of marital intimacy. Marriage provides an opportunity for multilevel exchanges of meaning. It provides the opportunity for communicating at increasingly deep levels about the things that matter most to husband and wife.

Howard J. and Charlotte H. Clinebell

"When two persons communicate, the verbal content of the message spoken and heard comprises only 7 percent of all that is transmitted. The tone of voice conveys an additional 33 percent. The other 60 percent is expressed by body posture, gestures, and facial signs."[1]

The subtleties of our nonverbal communication are scary. Body language—what we don't say, the way we look—transmits powerful and energetic messages in any relationship, but especially those within the marriage and family setting. We've all experienced those times when we have interpreted literally—we thought—the words and actions of our husband or wife, and then have responded according to our understanding, only to discover later in an angry or tearful scene that the signals were botched up badly and we were dead wrong.

The odds are very high at such times that we missed some pretty obvious, nonverbal signs that, had they been observed and accurately interpreted, could have assisted greatly in clearing the air of misunderstanding and latent hostility. By studied effort we may be successful now and then in disguising our true feelings through carefully selected words and a controlled tone of voice, but most of the time our nonverbal responses, if properly observed and interpreted, signal our real, below-the-skin feelings.

Telltale Signals

Recently Harriett and I were discussing the possibility of going either to Dallas or San Antonio with a group of friends. We talked about staying at our favorite hotel on the river in San Antonio and dining at one of the several colorful Mexican restaurants we enjoy. Then we could putter through the quaint shops along the Paseo del Rio and later relax through a pleasant evening at The Landing, listening to New Orleans-style jazz.

After exploring the San Antonio option fully, we discussed the Dallas idea: staying at the Fairmount Hotel and dining at the Pyramid Room, before rushing across town to take in a play at one of the theaters, with a final stop at the hotel floor show at the Venetian Room, before calling it a day—or morning—about 3:00 a.m.

Throughout our conversation I was being very careful not to express any personal preference. Actually, I felt quite proud and a bit smug over my outwardly agreeable nature: "Either one is all right with me. It's up to the rest of the crowd. I'll be happy either way."

But then Harriett gave me that know-all, see-all look that always raises my hackles and asked, "Why don't you want to go to Dallas?"

I protested, "It doesn't make any difference to me." And raising my voice half an octave, I insisted, "I said I'd be happy to go either place."

"I heard what you said, but the minute we started talking about going to Dallas you folded your arms tight across your chest, clenched your fists, crossed your legs, and wrinkled your forehead into a frown. You were resisting the whole idea."

Once again I had been tripped up by telltale body language even though I thought I was being so smooth. For me, at that moment, Dallas sounded like a run-and-rush weekend and twice as expensive as the alternative. On the other hand, I could visualize the informal scenario in San Antonio and knew that I would feel very relaxed and comfortable in that warm and soft Hispanic setting.

She was right. My defenses were up and I was resisting the whole idea of going to Dallas in spite of what I had said. And I signaled that message with arms folded tightly across my body like a baseball umpire hassling with an irate major league manager—a rather clear signal of resistance and defensiveness most of the time, at least with me. Irritated at being caught, I was getting a little petulant about the whole thing when we both started to laugh over the game that I was playing.

Even the casual student of body language realizes that crossed arms with hands clenched are usually signals that something has gone wrong, that communication has been choked off, and it might be well to reevaluate what and how something is being said. Drumming one's fingers on the chair arm or table, scratching one's nose, tapping the floor with a foot, negative and jerky head movements, leaning away from the speaker with a frown on one's face—these usually telegraph messages of indifference or anger or disagreement. Such actions have a way of speaking louder than specific words or even tone of voice. Here are caution signals blinking furiously, sending out messages that for some reason good, sensitive, and open communication is blocked and there's danger ahead.

Under normal circumstances none of us is inclined to think clearly when conflicting and negative emotions are coursing through our nerve endings. And it is just at these times when two people who love each other should apply the brakes, look deeply into each other's eyes, and say thoughtfully, "Just a minute, we're headed down a wrong track. I'm very uncomfortable about my feelings and I'm sorry for anything I've said or done that has irritated you. Let's back up and start over. I love you." Most of the time that will break the threatening cycle for us and open the door once again for two-way communication.

An awareness of kinesics—the study of how we communicate by physical gestures and mannerisms—will help most people over some rough spots. I know, for example, when Harriett is leaning toward me, her body obviously relaxed, her eyes looking straight into mine, that she is really hearing me and is open to what I am saying. I've gotten the "we're together on this" signal. My self-esteem and self-confidence soar, and I feel good about what's happening.

This is not to suggest that wives and husbands should set out to nitpick every body movement with a smug, know-it-all attitude or try to interpret every bat of an eyelash. An awareness of the frequent emotional give-aways of our body positions is not a Saturday night game of charades, for no particular body motion of itself is necessarily a trustworthy reflection of an inner feeling. Sometimes we fold our arms simply because the change of position feels good. But when several of the emotional indicators begin to send out signals at the same time, it is well to stop, look, and listen. Taking our example above, Harriett wasn't just reading my folded arms. She also noticed the accompanying telltale signals in my hands, legs, body, and forehead, and when questioned, I had protested my phony response too much. The signs were all there, and she knew it.

The Importance of Eye Contact

The art of establishing and maintaining close eye contact or linkage during a conversation or discussion makes an enormous difference in the impact of what we say as well as what we hear. In effect it says, "I care about you and am really interested in what you are saying. I want to make sure that I catch not only what you say but what you are feeling." Obviously, the kind of eye contact we're referring to here is not a fixed stare, which can be both rude and impertinent. And maintaining open and caring eye contact during any conversation does not preclude the relief of an occasional and polite glancing away. But it does involve that direct, unashamed linkage of eyes with far greater frequency than most of us achieve without conscious effort at first.

Ralph Waldo Emerson, the sage of Concord and one of the most perceptive interpreters of the feelings and thinking of people, expressed the importance of eye contact when he said, "The eyes of men converse as much as their tongues, with the advantage that the ocular dialect needs no dictionary but is understood the world over."

We've noticed that persons with professional training, such as performing artists, are particularly sensitive to the importance of eye contact in conversation. Almost without exception, in our experience, a trained actor or actress gives the impression in a conversation that only you are important and only what you are saying is worth listening to. How sincerely flattering! I recall well my first visit with Jane Withers, producer, actress, and former child motion picture star, when we had dinner together at an intimate little restaurant in Hollywood. The lilt in her voice, her contagious laugh, and her facial expressions and gestures signaled an interest in me as a person and in what I was saying. Within minutes I knew Jane was my friend, and her eyes relayed a message that made me feel worthwhile and important. We communicated, and even now I remember in detail much of what we talked about that night.

While I had been increasingly aware of the importance of eye contact to effective communication, that particular evening with Jane impressed me in a new and forceful way, and eye contact has become a conscious effort ever since. There is no doubt that this requires constant practice and must be worked at, but we have discovered that when we're at our best and are remembering to do what we know to do, our sending and receiving antennae are energized by the intimacy that flows out of eye contact. Try it; the rewards are rich!

Subtle Feelings Indicators

Almost always our facial expressions are dead giveaways to what is really going on consciously or unconsciously down deep inside of us. Irrespective of what we say, lips pressed together in a straight line, the jaw clenched hard, or the mouth twisted either into a sneer or a mocking smile betrays an uptight attitude and suggests a closed mind.

When Carl and Louise were discussing the kinds of things that trigger an argument between them, she told us, "I have a facial expression which I really am not aware of that ticks him off right then. That has started some really good fights." To which Carl responded, "She has a way of looking at me in a demeaning manner, like 'you dummy,' and I say, 'Don't look at me like that.' "

I have a telltale trait that I wasn't particularly conscious of on the surface, but which signals irritation to Harriett.

After putting up with it for years, she said one day, "I know you're upset, but I don't know what about." I protested, "What makes you say that? I'm not upset about anything." And she responded, "Yes, you are! You almost never whistle. But I've noticed that when you suddenly start bustling around with a blank, noncommittal expression on your face and whistle in a sort of low monotone, sooner or later it comes out that you're mad or upset about something."

While the whistle could be interpreted as a verbal signal, my silence about what was really bothering me was certainly a strong nonverbal indication of my feelings. And as Terry Hekker says, "The only inhumane weapon that should be outlawed by international convention is silence. Silence is very effective but inordinately cruel. Words wound but silence tears you apart."[2]

Scene 1—Ralph and Stella

When we walked into the Walker home, it felt good. It was obvious the family room was lived in, and even the collie dog seemed comfortable and at ease in his tail-wagging friendliness. Ralph and Stella, an energetic couple involved in a variety of side interests, gave every indication of having a good life. But in their twenty-six years of marriage it hadn't always been that way. Ralph remembered, "When we used to have disagreements, I would get quiet and pout. As I saw it, our discussions didn't get us anywhere, and I would withdraw into silence to show my displeasure. And then when Stella was depressed and ill, I felt like I was walking on eggs. Nothing I did was ever right."

Stella interrupted with, "My way of handling things was to leave the house and take a walk. When I announced that I was going for a walk, it was my way of communicating so he couldn't miss it that I was unhappy with him."

"But that's all past now," Ralph cut in. "In fact, some of our friends think we overdo it. Boy, if I could tell young married couples anything, or older ones for that matter, it would be to be frank, loving, honest, and open. Don't carry hidden agendas or excess baggage. Get it all out into the open. Silence, pouting, or running away never solves anything."

The Peril of Silence

After talking intimately with many people like Ralph and Stella Walker, we had the clear message that probably the most crippling form of nonverbal communication is the deadly pattern of retreating into silence, of pouting, in the inevitable times of disagreement which come to every couple. John Powell writes, "The pouting game is played by emotional children. The pouter cannot sit down and openly discuss interpersonal problems, usually because his position is irrational and he secretly knows it. He can scourge others emotionally by his silence, sad looks, etc., without having to tell them what is bothering him."[3]

Reuel Howe makes an incisive comment on the cancer of silence:

> Many relationships are destroyed because of accumulated resentments. The husband may have said something that irritates his wife. She says nothing. She bottles up her anger which daily gets worse. But she cannot talk about what really concerns her and she begins to fuss with him about little things. He retaliates and soon their love is lost in a jungle of hostilities.[4]

We are a part of a social society. We feed on our interactions with other people. From the first good morning until the last good night, we send out signals to loved ones, to colleagues, to the checker at the grocery store, to the waitress at the restaurant, to the attendant at the self-serve gas station, to the clerk at the local department store. These signals are a quiet cry for recognition, for acceptance, for assurance. Our moods soar at others' recognition and affirmation, and plunge at their silence. After all, silence signals rejection; it freezes us out. Silence indicates failure and eats away at our feelings of self-esteem; it tends to reduce us from person to thing.

A distinction must be drawn here, however, between the negative silence just referred to, which is destructive, and a *positive silence that is reconciling and healing*. Psychologist Wayne Oates of the University of Louisville, and a valued advisor to us, comments, "There is a need for silence that comes from having laid a problem to rest. The spouse who keeps 'harping' on an old issue, 'throwing it up' again and again, needs to learn the silence that comes from real forgiveness."

The Magic in Touching

It is often a rather humiliating experience to see ourselves as others see us. But the scenario in which Harriett and I play out the effects of our dammed-up communication is probably not untypical. There we are—two people sitting stiffly about ten feet apart, eyes downcast, not looking directly at each other, but being plenty vocal. It's only as we work toward understanding, sometimes rather stubbornly, that we find ourselves moving closer together physically.

Then when we seem to run out of words, Harriett may say, "I just want you to hold me." And with that we find ourselves in each other's arms because that's where we want to be. The disagreement is all but forgotten as we come together in the loving and caring that we really feel. Other times I'll reach out and take her hand, squeeze it, and say, "Honey, I love you," and the stormy scene begins to subside.

There is magic in touching. It is a powerful means of communication. But this, too, we believe, is an acquired art, because so many of us enter the marriage relationship without having experienced it ourselves or having seen our parents openly and physically express their love for each other.

Frances, a rather stout, emotionally bottled-up woman of forty-nine, commented, "I never saw or heard my father and mother express their feelings toward each other. I have no recollection of being hugged or cuddled by either my mother or father. In fact, my only memory of being touched was when I was spanked, and then my father would tell me it hurt him more than it did me. There was just no way I could buy that. This is why I found it so hard to show and express love for my husband or our children." How much this had to do with the tragic collapse of Frances' marriage three years earlier is open to question, but there was little doubt that this touch-starved person was still suffering from the crippling effects of an unfortunate and bewildering childhood.

In reflecting on her childhood, Harriett has no recollection of being hugged or caressed by either her mother or father. She does recall rather vividly asking to sit on her mother's lap while the funny papers were being read, and feeling rebuffed as she was told, "You may sit beside me but not on my lap; it hurts my legs."

Nothing is to be gained by pointing accusing fingers at our parents or grandparents who were the unfortunate victims of the culture and mores of their times. After all, their models for showing affection were their parents and grandparents, who were born into a time tainted by the remnants of a frontier mentality which characterized tenderness and displays of affection as weakness. Even in our lifetime, Roy Rogers didn't get to kiss the girl in any of his motion pictures for fear his manhood would be questioned. By contrast, he could pet and kiss Trigger on the nose without sacrificing his macho image. Such is our heritage. But the sooner we see it for what it is, the sooner we can be freed to give and receive the physical expressions of love we're all starved for. We agree with Walt Whitman when he wrote in *Hospital Visits*, "There is something in personal love, caresses, and the magnetic flood of sympathy that does, in its way, more good than all the medicine in the world."

Scene 2—Nancy and Ned

Nancy, an attractive forty-four-year-old wife and mother of three teenagers, was one of the few people we talked to who had warm recollections of being patted and cuddled as a child by both her father and mother. Their Hispanic heritage made it easy for them to be effusive and open. "Even now," she explained, "when my older brothers go home to visit my parents, they greet my father with big bear hugs just like they did when they were little boys. It's all very natural. But when Ned and I were married, he just didn't understand that. He seldom touched me unless he had sex on his mind. And he just couldn't understand why I wasn't turned on and ready to leave the dishes in the sink and run for the bedroom. I needed the assurance that comes from touching and caressing all the time—not just as a springboard to sex."

Ned explained, "I was raised in a narrow, restrictive, religious environment and never remember seeing or experiencing touching or loving in our home. My minister father railed at the evils of dancing, and ranted against everything that he was sure was going on in parked cars outside the dance halls or school gyms. He seemed to preach against anything I thought would be fun. I spent most of my boyhood on the sidelines except for church. Life was a serious and pretty deadly business, not to be enjoyed but endured. It seemed like no matter how hard I tried I never measured up. So I became sort of a loner and insulated myself against other people. I felt this was the only way I could avoid getting hurt. When I met Nancy, I was attracted by her openness and affectionate manner, but I didn't really know how to respond, and her family drove me up the wall. It has taken me twenty-two years to work through this and to break down even a little bit. But I keep working at it because it feels good, and Nancy says I'm 100 percent better than I was. I'm even beginning to enjoy being a part of her family."

Then after a rather long pause, Ned added, "You know, when I think about it very much, I get a little angry. I have a feeling I've missed a lot over the years. And it wasn't necessary. If only my parents had been able to share their feelings—if they had them, and I'm sure they did."

Fun and Games

A few years ago we read a fun suggestion by Dorothy Samuel which we like, and when we think to follow her advice, things get spiced up considerably around our house:

> No couple can avoid . . . irritations; any two persons sharing one house will get in each other's way from time to time. The closer and more intimate the association, the greater the opportunities for stumbling over each other and each other's peccadillos.
>
> So enjoy it! Don't squeeze by each other in the narrow passageway—bump into each other! Make passing as difficult as possible, extending rumps and elbows, jostling shoulders and hips. Exploit every

opportunity for 'fun and games' and the delicious sexual stimulation of the passing rub and the sensuous pressure.[5]

Why is it so easy to forget and take each other for granted? In the two years Harriett and I went together before getting married, we found all kinds of excuses to communicate by touching and brushing against each other—parked down at the beach or up in the hills, at church or walking down the streets of our little town. And it was especially great to snuggle close on a cold November night at the football game when a damp fog blanketed the whole Southern California coast.

One carryover from those times persists to this day. In church, whenever and wherever, when it comes time for the sermon, Harriett always slips her arm under mine and we hold hands. I'm sure there was a time when we didn't do this, but I don't remember it. There's something about it, though, that is never mechanical or routine. For us, it signals that everything is all right between us and with the world. It is a little thing, and some people might think it's sort of funny for a couple our age to hold hands in church, but it has become a symbolic touch, a ritual that is always new and fresh.

Yes, there *is* magic in touching. For in touching we give ourselves to the other person, and in so doing we affirm his or her worth and value as a person to us. There is that mystical something in each of us which cries out for reassurance, for affirmation. A pat, a squeeze, a caress, a touch signals, "You're O.K."; "I'm proud of you"; "I want you"; "I'm glad you're my wife (husband)."

We've come to suspect that loving, physical contact in all its forms is a powerful contributor toward a healthy and happy relationship and a loud and clear signal that all is well. But we have discovered in our research that for some people it may come naturally, while for others frequent, loving body contact—touching, patting, hugging—seems awkward. For this kind of person only time and overt effort can peel away the insensitive layers of a hurtful past until feelings are released and can be physically expressed with openness and abandon.

Scene 3—Hank and Katherine

Hank was a strong, silent type who, because of his background, just didn't seem able to verbally express his love for Katherine. He said he always felt awkward if he tried to pat or touch her in public or even when the two of them were alone. To which Katherine responded in a strident tone of voice, "The only time he touches me is when he wants to make love, and then he expects me to have an instant turn-on."

After a rather lively exchange, Hank admitted that a psychologist friend of his had suggested that he deliberately program himself to express his love and appreciation for Katherine six times a day every day. And he emphasized that this should include nonsexual pats and hugs. But Hank had protested that this would be too mechanical and he'd feel foolish.

"Try it and see," was Katherine's immediate response. "Deep down I know you still love me, but I need for you to tell me; I need the good feeling that would come from a touch or a caress. There is just no way a pat on the fanny, that isn't a clumsy invitation to bed, can be mechanical very long."

From all we've seen, heard, and felt, we think she was right. Touching can be learned and the process needn't be mechanical—at least for long. Bruce, another husband we talked to, said it for a lot of men, and women, too: "I had to learn to touch after I was married. It wasn't easy for me, but I desperately wanted to learn, and I know we've had a happier and richer married life as a result."

A Car Tells the Story

At times the things we surround ourselves with can make telling nonverbal statements about who we are and what we are feeling. On one particular Saturday morning the temperature had dipped to 21 degrees, but the chill factor, according to the morning weather report, hovered at around zero. Our half-city, half-country neighborhood just outside of Grand Rapids' east beltline, with its acre lots, prolific with huge oaks and spruce, rested under a heavy blanket of dry, powdery snow.

It was a day to stay inside, read a book, enjoy the sight and smell of oak logs crackling in the fireplace. But I had an itch that had to be scratched, so I bundled up, warmed up the car, and headed to the north side of town to the Dodge agency. Over the past weeks since my forty-eighth birthday I had convinced myself that it was time to buy a new car.

The warm showroom didn't offer any possibilities, so the salesman and I braved the outdoors and wandered through the lot of new cars. Every now and then we would stop and brush the snow off of one so I could examine it more closely.

Then I saw it! There was *my* car. A closer look told me that it wasn't quite right, but almost. And so I rushed home to pick up Harriett. I was sure she'd like what I found, but I wanted her in on the decision—that's the way it is at our house. Back we went across town to the Dodge lot, and after parking we headed straight for *the* car.

In the meantime the salesman had brushed all the snow off, and there it was—a sleek, fire-wagon red convertible with a stylish black top. Harriett looked at me, read the look on my face and my tone of voice, and calmly said, "It's beautiful. If you like it, let's buy it."

Both the salesman and I were delighted with her reaction. But then I explained that we couldn't take that particular car because I wanted my convertible to have factory air conditioning; we'd have to order another one from Detroit—same color, same everything, plus factory air conditioning. With this, the salesman's impression that he had a middle-aged nut on his hands could be clearly seen in the incredulous expression on his face. The last thing he had expected on that freezing cold day was to sell a red convertible—and one with air conditioning at that. But he recovered quickly, and the order was placed.

Three weeks and a telephone call later, I picked up my new, shiny, midlife-crisis red convertible, with its rich looking black top, factory air conditioning, and that incomparable new car smell. Did I feel good!

For me there seemed to be considerable truth to the notion that "persons required to contemplate psychologically pure-red" for a period of time were definitely stimulated through their nervous system—"blood pressure increases, respiration rate and heartbeat both speed up."[6] Red is perceived to have an exciting effect on the nervous system. And it certainly did on mine.

I'll always remember that car. We kept it four years and I never had the top down. The air conditioning came in handy, though, because a year or so after buying it we moved to Central Texas. But it was that car which communicated, nonverbally, a strong statement about me at the time I bought it. Out of my professional and midlife insecurities it broadcast some otherwise unexpressed feelings to Harriett, and anyone else who cared to listen: "Hey, here I am. I'm not over the hill. In fact, I haven't reached my peak yet. I may be forty-eight, but I've got young ideas. If you don't believe it, look at this red car."

The "Voice" of Color

The colors with which we surround ourselves and the way we dress under various circumstances can certainly be subtle means of communication between husband and wife. We have come to believe there is a connection between the color and style of the clothes we wear and our feelings. If I'm feeling up, feeling good about myself, at peace with the world and satisfied with the way things are going at the office, feeling in love with Harriett at the moment, the chances are pretty good that I'll have on my neatly tailored, light gray plaid suit, a soft gray shirt with French cuffs and black onyx cuff links, matching gray leather shoes, and a bright-colored tie which complements the outfit.

On the other hand, if I'm down, upset, feeling a bit rejected, a little mad at the world, then the brown, baggy suit is O.K., with brown tie and scuffed brown shoes, all sort of tumbled together carelessly in a bland and sterile, I-don't-care look.

And it works the other way around, too. When I come home after a busy and possibly frustrating day at the office and find Harriett in a perky, colorful outfit, I get the message that it's been a good day for her, she likes herself, her meeting that morning went well, she isn't annoyed with me. Immediately, I get a pick-up; I begin to feel better. Just her appearance can give me a lift and I start to feel more worthwhile. Both of us are very color sensitive— bright, warm colors bolster our spirits and tend to enhance our feelings of self-esteem. For both of us a statement is being made; an image is projected which brings into focus a partial reflection of how we feel about ourselves.

Wake Up to the 60 Percent

Perhaps the most sobering idea to cut across our thinking processes as we have tried to discover the ingredients of a long-term and fulfilling marriage is that *60 percent of what we express to our husbands or wives and to our children within the family setting is conveyed not by what we say, but by our body language,* by how we look and respond nonverbally to the flow of life around us. This fact is revealed in an awareness between people who love each other that there's nothing trivial about various body movements and positions, about our facial expressions, or about the colors we wear and surround ourselves with. In fact, the pulse of life is frequently felt in seeming trivialities. And a sensitivity to these subtle signals may well be the key that can unlock the door to the kind of understanding that leads to a lasting and exciting marriage relationship, in spite of less than perfect conditions.

Chapter Seven

The Adventure of Growing Together

Marriage is a process, a fluid relationship that assumes many different forms throughout the years; a relationship that is always either growing or deteriorating.　　　　Nancy Mayer

"If we don't change, we don't grow. If we don't grow, we are not really living. Growth demands surrender of security. It may mean giving up familiar but limiting patterns, safe and unrewarding work, values no longer believed in, relationships that have lost their meaning."[1]

"If you and your husband are vital, growing individuals different today from what you were yesterday, and if you can communicate this growth not only emotionally and philosophically but sexually, your marriage over the years will remain vital and creative."[2]

In these strongly worded statements from Gail Sheehy and Masters and Johnson, we come into blunt confrontation with a bald fact of marital life: *If a marriage is to last, to be exciting and adventurous, to be satisfying and fulfilling, the couples somehow will have to discover growth patterns that are mutually rewarding.* And while certain periods of married life seem more fertile for positive growth experiences than others, each stage provides its own particular set of challenges and opportunities.

The saying of wedding vows and the pronouncement of the minister that a relationship is launched signals a climactic moment when two people are united. But perhaps of even greater significance is the establishment of a relationship which has latent within it enormous opportunities for growth together and satisfaction as individuals and as a couple.

Early Conditioning

Up to the time of marriage most of us have moved through the childhood and adolescent cycles of life influenced and shaped by the teaching and conditioning of parents, of family life, and by social environment. We have passed through years fraught with the turmoil of intense physical, emotional, and sexual change and maturing as we have moved from dependency on parents and family to independence as persons. The headlong rush of change and growth and learning during our childhood and adolescent years has left most of us with a mixed bag of confused and conflicting emotions and feelings. This "is a time of extraordinary growth, but it is also a prelude to adult living. Its result is an immature individual making his entry into an adult world."[3]

Often, underneath the newly married couple's façade of almost reckless self-confidence comes a haunting realization: out of the stuff and debris of the learning and experiences of two not quite grown-up people, there is very little that has really prepared them to forge a new relationship. This is not to underrate the influence of our childhood and adolescent years—good or bad—in shaping our attitudes, actions, and patterns of relating throughout the rest of our lives.

We have talked with many people who have brought happy and positive feelings about the childhood and adolescent years into their adult married life. They felt loved and affirmed as children and carried forward no significant negative feelings about childhood discipline or being allowed to grow toward independence as persons. At the same time, we have known and talked with many more persons whose adult lives and marriage relationships have been adversely affected, and at times crippled, by a rigid, authoritarian mood in their childhood experiences, or a violent and humiliating form of discipline which tended to destroy one's sense of well-being and worth, or by an absence of warm and assuring expressions of love and affirmation.

But it isn't necessary for a person to remain emotionally imprisoned to this early conditioning. No one needs to be permanently enslaved to the past. And unless couples reach the beginnings of an understanding of this truth, the results can be devastating and will likely disfigure their marriage and family life. The tendency then is to repeat and act out the patterns of one's own childhood home life and inflict those same crippling attitudes and actions on mates and children. But, happily, we can change and grow as we mature to an understanding that the supreme cop-out in life is to blame, consciously or unconsciously, what and who we are on parents, childhood experiences, or the circumstances of any earlier stage in our lives.

The Ecstasy and the Agony of Survival

But, irrespective of childhood backgrounds, for most of us, our inexperience and lack of preparation for married life was bewildering. For Harriett and me it was only later that we came to understand and cope with La Rochefoucauld's observation, "Each age of life is new to us; no matter how old we are we are still troubled by inexperience." But it is out of this inexperience and newness that a young married couple begins to discover, possibly unconsciously at first, the adventure of growing both as individuals and as two people committed to each other. Thus can begin a process of growth that will give direction and purpose and unity during each of the following life cycles.

Harriett and I suspect that our marriage is not unlike that of most couples, in that it began at the lower end of what Daniel Levinson and his research associates have labeled the "early adulthood period"—the ages of seventeen to forty-five.[4] During those early years we had little, if any, concept of what was involved in the growth process of marriage. We certainly wish now that we'd had even a little understanding about how to begin the growth process. But intuitively we managed somehow to bridge the first difficult year of adjustment, and we then muddled through the next eight or ten years by majoring pretty much on the physical side of our relationship. These were years of getting to know each other, of pressing for some kind of a blend between two independent personalities, of struggling to find a satisfying kind of physical and sexual intimacy—evidently a very normal experience with most young couples.

As with the majority of people, those years were further involuted by the birth of one child, our only daughter. While that was a supremely happy and planned-for occasion, it brought a radical change in our lifestyle for which we were not remotely prepared. And at times we felt more than a little frightened and confused by the changes and the new problems. It was during those same years that we were also struggling to find some form of identity not only as a couple but as persons, and to establish our place in a world that at times seemed dreadfully hostile and cold.

These were years of petty arguments and conflict about money, forgotten dates, disappointing Christmas and birthday gifts, working long hours, and being too tired for sex. Feelings were hurt by forgetting to say "I love you," and short-tempered responses were engendered by anxiety over money, which was always in short supply. Our security was threatened, too, by the possibility of my being drafted and sent overseas. And patience seemed always to be worn thin by the pressing demands of a job, or a car that broke down frequently, or by forgetting to put gasoline in the tank and then running out in heavy evening traffic.

It was survival, not growth, that consumed our every living moment of time and every volt of energy. While we exerted enormous energy to succeed, there was little conscious effort to grow. And yet as we ricocheted between ecstasy and agony, through our commitment to each other, as best we understood it, a foundation was somehow being set for growth patterns that could be built on later and would ultimately become a conscious part of our lifestyle.

Awareness of the Need to Grow

As with most couples of our generation, and even now in the 1990s, we had married "for life." (Yes, in spite of the gloomy statistics on the breakdown of marriage, current polls indicate the majority of young couples still marry for life.) Maintaining that life commitment will be made far easier the earlier in their relationship a couple begins to pay conscious attention to mutual growth. But it is usually only in their thirties and early forties that couples first become aware of the importance of fortifying their commitment to each other in this way. The physical and sexual experiences become no less important, but most people, unless they have been scarred or shattered emotionally, carry deep within them the desire for a satisfying companionship and love. Thoughtful planning together can ward off the possibility of future complacency or boredom and open the way for rich and fulfilling experiences in midlife.

This is an important time of life, too, for confronting the reality that maintenance is far more essential to the preservation of a marriage than even to a house or car or any other material gadget we may happen to own and hold dear. Harold Lyon underscores this idea:

> Most devices that we purchase don't need as much upkeep initially as they do when they begin to get older. They do require maintenance if they are going to last for a lifetime, however, and relationships are certainly no different. New ones don't seem to need much maintenance. But if they are to be lifetime relationships, maintenance—the sharing of goals, strengths, barriers, and fears—must occur regularly.[5]

At this time, as well, we can begin to see that a relationship cannot remain set or constricted; otherwise stagnation develops. Rather, a creative and healthy relationship is more like the kaleidoscopes we played with as children—each turn produces a change that is potentially beautiful and exciting, unless our vision is limited by the familiar and by an insistence that the past, whether pleasant or not, is to be preferred to the unknown of the future.

Attitudes Toward Growth

We have discovered, however, in sharing in the experiences and confidences of the people we've talked with, most of whom range in age between forty and sixty-five (the "middle adulthood" period, according to Levinson),[6] there are strong differences between partners in their feelings and attitudes about who and what they really are as persons and as married couples.

Some of them appeared to be quite relaxed and at ease, and talked freely about their life together. They were open with their descriptions of periodic flareups, vigorous and vocal misunderstandings, hurt feelings over apparent slights or thoughtlessness, and irritating traits or habits acquired over the years. There were frank admissions of occasional bouts with overwhelming feelings of insecurity and anxiety. And there was a recognition in some instances of dreams unrealized—thickening bodies, thinning hair, less energy than in earlier years. But these couples seemed to have discovered something within their relationship and experience which enabled them not just to cope with stressful circumstances, but to move and grow through their days together with confidence and a sense of adventure.

Then we talked with the Archie Bunker-types who seemed to be uptight with themselves and each other. Their asides and comments were barbed, tinged with sarcasm or bitterness. They gave the impression of feeling cynical, negative, or gloomy about their marriage relationship and about life in general. The world, according to these doomsayers, was falling apart morally and politically, and they seemed sure that some form of cataclysmic Armageddon was just around the corner.

And we talked with others who appeared to be just plain bored with each other, disenchanted with themselves and with what was going on around them. There was a flatness, a grayness, a plastic lack of vitality that we found depressing. They gave every indication of being trapped in dull and unsatisfying marriages but apparently feared the consequences of doing anything about it, or had become too settled and apathetic to really care. And some of those we talked with had obviously, by their own admission, set out to compensate for less than satisfying relationships by going their separate ways with each doing his or her own thing. More questions arose:

- What made the difference?
- Why has the rate of divorce increased dramatically among couples who have been married twenty or more years?
- Why do so many couples seem bored with each other?
- What can be done, after years of being together, to keep a marriage from turning rancid and stale, and becoming a stage for bickering, put-downs, and explosive scenes?
- What kinds of actions and attitudes seem to produce a warm and happy relationship that lasts?
- What does their earlier and present growth as individuals and as a couple have to do with their attitudes and behavior now?

We suspected we'd find some clues to the answers if we looked further. And we did.

Scene 1—Dottie and Millie

With disarming candor, Dottie, who had been married at nineteen, said, "I think turning forty was the hardest thing I ever did. It was terribly traumatic for both my husband and me. He had such a fear of being called a grandfather, and he resented it when I would tell somebody how old our children were. Then I had this thing about having to stay young in order to keep him—that was a constant worry to me. I used all the nonwrinkle creams I could find and starved myself most of the time to keep my good figure and wear a size 6 dress."

Dottie had kept her good figure, and the sags and bulges, if any, were well concealed. But she reflected an aura of brittleness that offset her attractive physical attributes. The tension crease above her nose and the fidgety body movements seemed to reveal intense feelings of dissatisfaction with herself and her marriage relationship. When I asked her to describe her marriage growth patterns, she responded, "Oh, I'm afraid we've grown apart instead of together. We used to enjoy doing things together, but not much any more." She and her husband were apparently victimized by creeping separateness.

Millie came at our questions from an entirely different perspective. "I never worried about my age because I knew that every day I got older Edward did too—and so did my friends. I've looked at a couple of my girlfriends who have no gray hair and thought, should I color my hair? At a distance they look so much younger than I do. But if I can stay happy, that's what counts."

Several years ago our attention was arrested by the "quote of the week" in the *Washington Post*. It was made by a forty-year-old Claudia Cardinale, who was pregnant by an Italian film director whom she had decided not to marry. Her words stand in contrast with both Dottie's and Millie's: "Marriages break up because people get to know each other too well. Boredom is the death of love . . . and habit kills romance."

While there is obviously more than a hint of truth in part of Miss Cardinale's statement, we have to ask:

- Can a growing, maturing married couple get to know each other *too* well?
- Is there room for boredom in a growing relationship?
- Does the marriage relationship inevitably lose its zip and deteriorate into dull routine, a habit-plagued relationship which kills romance?

The Meaning of Growth

We attempted to work through these questions in light of our own experience and the feelings of the many people we've talked with. In that struggle we were driven back again and again to our thinking and discussions on growth and what it means in the marriage relationship. We have come to believe that in large measure our attitudes—our actions and reactions toward ourselves, our mates, and to just about everything around us at each stage of life, but especially at midlife or middle adulthood—are determined by our growth and development patterns. *And growth, as we understand it, hinges on flexibility, openness to change and new ideas, a curious and inquiring eagerness to learn, a commitment to adventurous living.*

But as we talked with both married couples and divorced persons in our interview-research, an intriguing pattern began to emerge. In response to our questions about their growth experiences as persons and as married couples, only about one in eight was able to respond specifically. The vagueness of their answers seemed to indicate that little thought had been given to the importance of developing and working out life-broadening and enriching activities that would open the way toward their growth both as individuals and as married couples.

This rather alarming lack of positive response surprised us at the time, because undoubtedly most of us would agree intellectually with the need to grow as persons. But it is not what we *know* but what we *do* that gives direction to our lives and brings happiness, heartbreak, or sterility. We know there aren't easy or precise answers to the questions we've asked ourselves. But out of the diverse marriage stories we've listened to for the past years, and out of our own marriage biography, we believe we've discovered some very practical and useful ideas that can guide us toward finding greater fulfillment and joy through living in a growing relationship with our husbands or wives.

An unfortunate fact of life, at least in our American culture, is that too often little or no conscious attention is given to our growth as persons and as couples during the first twenty or so years of married life. This neglect can usually be credited to the rough-and-tumble scramble to make a life as a married couple caught in the tensions of raising children, while at the same time, either by necessity or choice, engrossed in the frenetic pursuit of two careers.

This simply means that as couples move into their forties and fifties, and the demands of children and the career struggles level off a bit, there is a good chance that two "strangers," who've been sharing the same bed during those years, suddenly find themselves adrift. In all probability they do not have a reservoir of individual or shared interests to fill the vacuum, nor the talent and will to contribute to their own growth and toward the benefit of society. Perhaps even more tragic is the inattention, in most instances, to learning how to experience genuine enjoyment, enrichment, and fun on a day-to-day basis. And, usually, little effort has been made to build a widening circle of rich and interesting friendships. What a needless and sad lack of balance!

Living Longer with Each Other

But we have come to understand a little better how this can happen because of an awareness that we are living in a time of immense and rapid change. After all, in past societies there was little cause for concern about a person's preparation for growth or even for living much beyond forty or fifty. By the time the last child was on his or her own and out from underneath the family shelter, there was a strong likelihood that the marriage relationship had already been fractured by the death of either the husband or wife. In other words, our heritage—or as Carl Jung termed it, our "collective unconscious"—has not prepared us for the modern-day phenomenon of living on into the sixties, seventies, and eighties with the accompanying possibilities of a marriage relationship of twenty-five, thirty, or forty years.

The reality of this phenomenon is corroborated by the research of Professor Clifford H. Swensen, Jr., of Purdue University and other researchers whose work he has studied. Their findings indicate that until the last fifty years or so, one partner in the typical marriage died about the time the last child left home, so that few marriages survived beyond the children's departure. In other words, the last fifty years have witnessed the development of a whole new stage of marriage that had existed before in relatively few cases.[7]

Stay Open to Change

And so, in whatever the stage of life we find ourselves as we seek personal and marital enrichment, our attention returns again and again to the importance of consciously working to experience growth in our lives. And growth of any kind comes first with an openness to change—to an acceptance of new things, new activities, and new ways of thinking. Unfortunately, most of us have to overcome a built-in resistance to experimenting with and testing new and different ideas and patterns for living. This is especially true as we grow older and the friction of inertia becomes more of a controlling force in our lives.

Our close friend and colleague, Bruce Larson, expresses it well when he writes:

Even the most adventuresome of us—those of us who are the least committed to and defensive of the past—still fear change. I've read that people who have been faced with freezing to death in the snow experience a cozy warm feeling that seduces them into inactivity. But to survive, a person must shake off this wonderful, comfortable feeling which leads to death and start to act by changing position frequently, by forcing activity. To stay alive during long exposure to freezing conditions, one has to go against instinctive feelings. To think the way we always have, to act in old patterns is non-threatening and comfortable, but it lulls us toward a frightening death of the soul. To stay alive we must be people on the move, alert to the exciting opportunities of change.[8]

And sociologist Jack Balswick, formerly of the University of Georgia and now with Fuller Theological Seminary, underscores this whole idea: "I firmly believe that human personality can change. We do ourselves a disservice when we think that we are born with a certain personality type which determines the way we respond to others. We human beings are dynamic, adaptable, and capable of change."[9]

Developing Trust

How can a person and a couple meet this challenge of being on the move and open "to the exciting opportunities of change?" Again, each of us must struggle to find answers satisfactory to ourselves. Obviously, no one can or should attempt to prescribe specifically for someone else. However, we believe there is one ingredient, at least, that is an essential part of the change and growth patterns of every married couple without exception: *being open and trusting with each other*. And in marriage, as in any relationship, openness is not a state of being that two people drift into haphazardly. Rather, it evolves from attitudes of mutual trust and confidence—confidence in ourselves first of all, and then confidence in our spouses. Masters and Johnson affirm this need by observing, "Marriages may grow, or fail to grow, depending on whether the husband and wife develop greater trust in each other, [and] greater confidence in themselves."[10]

When a husband and wife trust one another, they find it unnecessary to lie or to be deceptive, even about little things in their day-to-day experiences. Being open and honest creates a climate free of hidden agendas and suspicions, and it signals a growing together and a growing up that is essential to a rich and fulfilling relationship. Dr. Paul Tournier offers this promise out of his life and experience as a counselor and psychiatrist: "As soon as a husband and wife have the courage to be completely open with one another, whatever the cost, their marriage becomes once more a wonderful adventure."[11]

Adventure in Growth

Marriage is a daring adventure or it is nothing—an adventure in growth, in change, in broadening horizons, in breaking out of the rut of the familiar and into the excitement of doing new things together. This is usually a painful and threatening experience and takes courage and time. As Harriett describes what happened to us as we fought our way out of the doldrums and ruts of dull routines, perhaps our process and experiences will prove helpful.

"A statement by Flannery O'Connor has always impressed me, 'Conviction without experience tends to be harshness.' Believe me, I have strong convictions and feelings about the importance of growth, especially during the thirties and forties—those years leading up to and including the mid-life experience. But my convictions are mellowed by how unprepared I felt and the resultant hurt and agony I lived with for several years.

"Today, articles appear regularly in magazines calling women's attention to the importance of preparing for the time when sounds of children no longer add spice to your day, and you find yourself alone, utterly alone, with just your husband. But when *I* faced that traumatic time, I hadn't had the benefit of articles like that, so I was totally unprepared. And coincident with this life change was the jarring of a drastic move. After half a lifetime we left Southern California and moved to the upper Midwest for professional reasons. Floyd and I experienced the trauma of separation for the first time from our much loved daughter, who, after completing college, was establishing herself in the profession for which she was trained.

"As I sat alone in our new suburban home with its parklike surroundings, I felt terribly lonely. Here I was in a new city in a new state, without friends or family or the comfortable support of a familiar church. And for the first two or three months especially, at around five o'clock in the afternoon, I missed the familiar sound of our daughter's car pulling into the garage and the friendly slam of the back door as she entered the house.

"These were painful weeks and months—it was a time of trying to sort out feelings and values and priorities. And while Floyd was aware of my needs and was sympathetic with my feelings, his career change absorbed all of his energy and skill and most of his time. For many women this would have been the time for moving into a career opportunity outside the home as a means of regaining purpose and fulfillment. But I had just closed out twenty years in the work world which began when Floyd went back to school after we had been married seven years. I just didn't want to work any longer.

"All of this forced Floyd and me to sit down together and reevaluate our lives and goals. We admitted to each other that we had gotten pretty dull and predictable and that the ruts of routine seemed almost too deep to climb out of. I remember reading a book by James Peterson at about that time which focused in on exactly what we needed: 'If the couple are to make up for the gap left by their children's departure, they have to substitute new patterns of activity for those that previously involved the entire family, as well as to renew emotional commitments often forgotten or directed towards the children.'[12]

"So we decided together to shake loose and do some of the things we had always dreamed of doing in our earlier years. Many of them we would do together, but there were also some things we each needed to do on our own. It was important that neither of us become victims of emotional claustrophobia. And with this discussion and decision we moved out into what, up to that time, was to be the most exciting period of growth in our adult lives.

"For me, the first step was a planned program of reading—novels, biographies, nonfiction. I have always loved reading, and as time has passed it has become one of my greatest pleasures. Books—of history, culture, and people—have enriched my life and broadened my outlook. My reading, which usually involves at least two books a week, has had an immeasurable influence in the growth of my life and marriage, and I hope it has made me a more interesting conversationalist and person.

"Travel has been an equally enriching experience to us. Today's news on television and in the newspapers about what is happening in England, Germany, Italy, Greece, Turkey, Mexico, and other countries is more alive to me because of the places we've visited—a part of our deliberate decision to do and see new things. Our lives have been greatly enriched as we have tried to feel and absorb the culture and customs of people in various parts of the world. We've learned to appreciate the food and drink of these countries, and we find ourselves experimenting frequently with foreign dishes which add excitement to our dinners together. Here, too, we have discovered fun times of growth, of openness to new tastes and smells and experiences.

"At forty-five Floyd took up golf for the first time and a few years later I, too, took lessons, and we've spent hundreds of happy hours together and separately, following that little white ball around over eighteen holes of fairways, roughs, and greens. Neither of us has ever been particularly proud of our scores. But in addition to the fun and relaxation, Floyd's general knowledge of golf opened up a new door for him to write a book with Gary Player, a world golf favorite and champion and a person we both came to admire greatly as a friend. In fact, over the years we formed many warm and new friendships in and around the golf course and through related activities.

"About the time Floyd became heavily involved with golf, I took bridge lessons and became absorbed in this fascinating and frustrating game. Floyd gave it a try but decided it wasn't for him. This means that every week or so a bridge game is my time to be with and enjoy certain choice women friends. I also tried knitting, but that was a fiasco. I learned to knit and purl, but that was about all. I tried to knit a sweater, but it ended up being knee length, and there was about six inches difference in the length of the arms. That was a learning experience which didn't take.

"Shortly after we moved to the Midwest we tried another new thing that we had always wanted to do—ballroom dancing. There we were—two middle-aged people with two left feet that didn't seem to want to go in the right direction. But with the help of patient teachers and partners, we moved beyond the 'businessman's shuffle' and acquired at least a working mastery of most of the steps required for a full and enjoyable evening of music and fun. Since moving to Texas we've even come to appreciate the intricacies of square dancing—a great favorite in our part of the country.

"Throughout all of these new experiences which have enriched our lives in so many ways, Floyd and I have tried regularly to assume new tasks and roles in our church life. Spiritual growth happens to be a very important part of our life together, and so we have insisted on finding new expressions for our faith and service in the church today."

Expanding Ego Boundaries

Obviously, our odyssey as Harriett has described it—and it is still going on—has been right for us. But that doesn't mean we've always had smooth sailing. There have been some tight-lipped moments on the dance floor when one or the other of us kept missing a step or forgot a routine. I've gotten short-tempered more than once over what seemed like eighteen holes of roughs on the golf course. And, believe me, I blush to recall some of my antics at the bridge table.

But most kinds of growth emerge from moments of pain and trial and error. All of the activities we have tried have called for flexibility and new thinking on our part. None has demanded excessive financial involvement after our priorities were established. In the process we have grown together and, hopefully, have become more interesting people. Harold Lyon expressed it well in his book *Tenderness and Strength:*

People who are truly strong are able to flow toward each other. They can mix and merge their strengths, and they can open up spaces for each other to grow into, and for the relationship as a whole to expand into. The ability to do this requires a prior willingness to move beyond one's position and to expand one's own ego boundaries.[13]

As we work at expanding our ego boundaries, we find that many of our beliefs are less rigid; we can better tolerate the inevitable ambiguities of life.[14] It is in throwing off our rigidities that we become able in our relationships to accept the differences in our spouses, to give them room to function as separate individuals rather than trying to mold them into carbon copies of ourselves. As Dr. Paul Tournier says, "It is the very differences in our character, tastes, habits, prejudices, and convictions which oblige us to a greater effort to understand each other. These in turn lead to further growth in both of us."[15] In the flowing and growing together process that frequently occurs with couples who seem to be opposites, the exciting discovery is made that *growth involves the deliberate doing of new things*. And these bring fresh interests into our lives and experiences.

New Growth Discoveries

Throughout our study and research we've discovered individuals and couples who, like ourselves, have been wakened to fresh growth opportunities and activities which fit their own style.

- At fifty-two, Barbara and Jim Wilson bought their first small and not very expensive greenhouse. Now, most of Barbara's spare moments are spent in planting and nurturing seedlings and cuttings. And their manicured and colorful landscaping reflects the results of this newly discovered interest.

- Art and Betty Langden developed an almost neurotic passion for fishing after both were forty. Until then they had thought a spinning reel was just a later variation of the tops they had spun as children. Theirs was a great and at times distasteful learning process. Betty forced herself to get over feeling queasy at handling worms, grasshoppers, wriggling minnows, and the smelly stink bait that Texas catfish seem to find irresistible at least some of the time.

- Frank Butler expanded his world by linking up with a couple of friends to read books and articles into a recorder, producing cassette tapes for the visually handicapped people in their town. His wife, Susan, didn't think her voice was suitable for recording, so on the nights Frank is recording, she spends her time volunteering on the receiving desk at a local hospital.

Photography, learning to speak Spanish or German at night school, acting in civic theater productions, rock hunting, gourmet cooking, playing dominoes, cooking for Meals on Wheels, writing—the opportunities for growth activities are limitless to the innovative and caring couple who deliberately set out to share in an interesting, fulfilled, and happy life together.

Gay Talese, a widely-read author on the American scene, in anticipating sexual and marriage trends in the coming years, suggests that men and women "will become more equal partners in pleasurable and profitable pursuits and will become more able to appreciate themselves and to be alone. As a result, a man will find the same woman interesting for a long period of time. Marriages will be stronger."[16]

Growth Through Friendships

Another vital area of importance is the broadening of one's circle of friendships as a positive step toward growth both as an individual and as a couple. We have observed that the better-adjusted and happily married couples we talked with admitted that they worked constantly at the task of maintaining and building a broad network of close and intimate friendships. By contrast, those couples who were obviously dissatisfied and unhappy with themselves and their marriage could account for no close or intimate friends. Some even said they did not have one person with whom they could be completely open and themselves.

This interesting observation brought to mind our own deficiency in this area during the first twenty years of our marriage. Though we had made an occasional stab at building friendships, for the most part we lived self-sufficient, self-centered, and ingrown lives—much too reclusive. But during the reevaluation period Harriett referred to, we confronted this stunting lack in our lives. This was painful for me because of a rather frightening social shyness and insecurity I had always felt. The crippling fear was always present that if people got to know the real me, they wouldn't like what they found. The thought of possible rejection was more than I thought I could handle.

But Harriett gave me the support I needed, and together we consciously determined to come out of our shells and give other people a chance. Slowly, and at times with intense feelings of uncertainty, we opened up ourselves to others. True, there were occasions when it didn't seem to work, but most of the time it did. And as the years passed we have discovered an overwhelming richness through an ever-widening network of lasting friendships with other people and couples. Today, a wide circle of warm and interesting and diverse friendships is certainly high on the list of steps that have brought zest and excitement to our own marriage relationship.

Our feelings and findings about the importance to marriage of the enriching quality of intimate friendships were confirmed by psychologist and family counselor, Dr. Alan L. McGinnis. In a talk before a service club, he said, "We have so emphasized sexual and romantic relationships that friendship has been neglected. I think we suffer for that." He further contended that many of the people he counsels do not have a circle of close friendships. "As a result they tend to have more problems with their children and their marriages than most people. . . . All of us need to cultivate a handful of people who know the worst about us and still like us."

Growth: A Deliberate Decision

Without intending to belabor the point unduly, we want to stress the fact that we do not drift into becoming interesting to our husbands or wives or families or friends by accident. Rather, it comes as a deliberate decision to expand our interests and horizons, to welcome change and new patterns of thinking, to aggressively pursue new and different interests and things to do on a regular and planned basis. And in the process we move toward becoming more interesting to ourselves and others because of our increasing depth and richness at the core of our lives—an outgrowth of our inner strength. Rollo May hints strongly at this in writing, "One person with indigenous inner strength exercises a great calming effect on panic among people around him. This is what our society needs—not new ideas and inventions, important as these are, and not geniuses and supermen, but persons who can *be;* that is, persons who have a center of strength within themselves."[17]

Chapter Eight

Surviving the Child-Rearing Years

It's hard to juggle with valuables, Lord—
   to keep so many plates in the air,
   children,
   husband,
   work,
     friends—
There's such delicate timing involved.
Help me to keep them in balance, Lord.
In careless hands
People I love
   could shatter, too.

Marilee Zdenek

"The stress of living with one another still represents one of the greatest causes of distress."[1] To the about-to-be-married or newly-married, these words by Dr. Hans Selye, world authority on stress, may seem like a gross and possibly cynical overstatement. But to anyone who has been married for long, there is immediate agreement as to the lurking presence of stress in the relationship.

As a matter of fact, stress language seems to dominate our vocabulary. We feel the stress and distress of inflation, the threat of war, of changing moral values, and of the bewildering demands of relentless change in our lifestyles—all of these areas represent a plunge into the threatening unknown. And so it should come as no surprise to any of us that marriage, the closest of all human relationships, is constantly confronting stressful circumstances. But that isn't all bad!

The Two Sides of Stress

In his remarkable little book *Stress Without Distress*, Dr. Selye points out that "stress is the spice of life." He urges us to use stress as a positive force for personal achievement and happiness. Since it is clear that we can't avoid stress in our complex world, it is important that we learn to adjust and adapt to it. Dr. Selye continues with penetrating insight, "The great handicap of early students of this topic was their failure to distinguish between *distress*, which is always unpleasant, and the general concept of *stress*, which, in addition, also includes the pleasant experiences of joy, fulfillment, and self-expression."[2]

What a helpful idea! In and of itself, stress is neutral. Stress has to do with change, not the direction of change. People can have positive and creative experiences and still be stressed and respond to it in terms of their own coping mechanisms. It's how we handle a stressful situation that determines whether it turns into a pleasant and growing experience or becomes distressful and unpleasant. As with the formation and development of most of our attitudes, we are the key; it is what *we* decide to do that determines the outcome. This whole idea came into focus for Harriett and me several years ago in a way that we'll never forget.

A Tale of Stress and Distress

Early one June morning while it was still dark, we joined two couples and headed to northern Michigan for a canoe trip on the Pere Marquette River. Our friends were experienced in this sort of thing, but we'd never been in a canoe before. In fact, I didn't know the front end from the back. Even though we had been assured that there was nothing to it, I found myself tensing up as we drove along through the black morning. But I kept telling myself that this could be a learning experience which might bring a new sense of adventure into our lives.

As the darkness faded into the dim pewter light which carried the promise of daylight, my anxiety began to recede. And then when the sun flared above the eastern horizon, feelings of well-being seeped through my thoughts, pushing out dark, negative attitudes. The lush green of the countryside coupled with the clear, astringent morning air gave me the needed lift—I felt sure I could master almost anything on a day like this.

After an hour and a half we pulled off the highway into a narrow side road which meandered down to a clearing at the edge of the river. It was a breathtaking sight, straight out of a scenic postcard. The adrenalin began to flow, and even the sight of the three canoes perched on the bank failed to dampen my enthusiasm.

In a short time our lunches and gear were stowed away, and after five minutes of instruction on what to do and how to paddle, we pushed out into the current which was moving sluggishly at this point. Our daughter, Sherrill, sat at the back of the canoe, Harriett took over the center spot, and I was manning the oar in the front. For a few minutes everything went well, and during that short time I conjured up visions of early Indians paddling silently down the river as it cut through the dense forests which lined the banks. In my imagination I pictured Pere Jacques Marquette, the seventeenth century Jesuit missionary to the Indians, making his way along this river which now bore his name.

Shortly, though, I was jarred back to the present: "Why don't you do what you're supposed to do up there?"

Sherrill called out. My eyes cleared and, sure enough, instead of moving down the middle of the river we were headed straight for one of the banks. In a flash of panic I did what I thought I was supposed to do, but in a few moments we were pointed toward the opposite bank.

From that moment on I forgot all about Indians and Pere Marquette—every volt of energy was concentrated on trying to keep the canoe headed in the right direction. But I was lucky if we went fairly straight for a hundred yards before the zigzagging from one bank to the other began again in spite of all my efforts. At times we got so close to the bank that branches from the overhanging trees scratched our faces and arms even though we scrunched down as low as we could.

From the back of the canoe I was getting angry noises from Sherrill, and from the middle, Harriett, looking like Cleopatra in a straw hat banded with bright yellow feathers, was sending up strongly worded advice. There was no doubt about it—creative stress was getting close to becoming distress. But I was determined to maintain control and keep up my rational maneuvers, which were supposed to compensate for our erratic tendencies and adapt to the flow of the river. It was a grim yet comical scene, but finally, relief was in sight when we saw that our friends ahead had pulled onto a sand bar for lunch.

"How far did we come this morning?"

"Fifteen miles. We're just halfway."

My spirits took a nosedive—fifteen more miles of this? Nobody had warned us that it was to be a thirty-mile jaunt. But when lunch was over, we pushed out again with fresh determination to conquer the canoe and the Marquette. For whatever reason, our route seemed a bit less erratic than it had been in the morning. But I was still tense even though things seemed to be under partial control—at least some of the time.

The afternoon wore on, and about three o'clock our friends called back with the good news that we had just one more mile to go. The Marquette had widened and was flowing rapidly now. And after about another half mile the river curved to the left. As we moved into the turn, I saw a fisherman, dead ahead, waist deep in the water. We were headed straight for him, and I paddled furiously trying to avoid him. The front of the canoe missed him by three feet, but as we swung around, we clipped him with the tip of the back end.

He was too surprised to say a word, but the look on his face spoke volumes. All I could mutter was, "Excuse me, sir," as I paddled hard to get away from there as fast as possible. But my control was gone. My coping mechanism was shattered, and the creative stress I'd been struggling with all day exploded into distress. I'd had it! Here I was trying to be a nice congenial guy, and that canoe had made a fool out of me. I didn't like it one bit. Gone was the beauty of the day and the sense of achievement that we had made it this far. And to make matters worse, I wasn't too popular with Harriett. And Sherrill was especially unhappy about the scratches on her face and arms, because she was getting married in a few days and, naturally, wanted to be beautiful and unscarred.

With teeth-gritting determination I headed toward the bank where our friends were waiting. We made it; I'm not sure how. They said we had come thirty miles; but with all of our zigzagging, I knew our canoe had traveled at least fifty miles. Turning toward the river for one last look, I stared for a few minutes and watched it flow along westward toward its outlet in Lake Michigan. It was there I made a solemn vow: "As long as I live, I'll never step foot inside a canoe again." And I haven't! But we've often wondered, as we've thought back on that episode, just what kind of a story that amazed fisherman told his wife when he got home that night.

Now that we can reflect on that canoe trip with a bit more objectivity, we have come to see a powerful living principle at work which has an influence on all of our relationships, but especially on marriage. For twenty-nine miles of the trip the creative stress I felt kept us going; in spite of an erratic course, we were moving toward our goal. And even though we're still anti-canoe, feelings have mellowed to the point of realizing that my problems that day were brought on not by the canoe but by my overcompensation and overreaction.

Each time we got off course I overreacted with frantic paddling and concentrated too vigorously on the immediate problem. In the process I lost sight of the long-term goal for the day—to absorb the exquisite beauty of the tree-lined river, to enjoy the relationship with our friends, and to participate in a new learning adventure. And so, when faced with the climaxing crisis of the day—clipping the fisherman—I blew it in one distressful explosion.

Reactions to the Stress Question

In our conversations with the many people whose reactions and experiences gave meaning and life to our thinking, we talked frankly about the stresses and distresses which, in varying degrees, are common to most of us. What are they? What can we learn from them? And how can they be handled creatively? Or, how do we mishandle them? In most instances the responses were quite varied. But almost 100 percent of the people answered an unqualified *yes* to these more specific questions:

- Do you feel that raising children tends to put a strain on marriage?
- Is marital satisfaction reduced during those "terribly tired thirties," child-raising years?

Scene 1—Sam and Evelyn

The Goldens had welcomed us into their split-level home on Atlanta's north side with a warmth and friendliness that put us at ease and set the stage for a relaxed conversation. Sam and Evelyn let us know they were proud of their family, and Jewish roots and traditions seemed to be embedded deeply into their life patterns. It was obvious from their comments that children, parents, and grandparents, were much loved and cared for. Theirs was not the contemporary nuclear family model of mother, father, and children (a phenomenon of the middle and late twentieth century). Rather, they were a comfortable part of a loyal, extended family. One son still lived at home, the other four sons lived close by, as did both sets of parents and Evelyn's grandparents.

Had raising those five boys put stress on their relationship as a married couple?

"I'll say it did," Evelyn responded firmly. "I can still remember the terrible fatigue I felt when the boys were small. There was no way I could keep up with all the work. I was on the run all day long, and by the time Sam would get home from the office I was dead tired, too tired to talk, too tired for sex—and it seemed like he was always ready. Naturally that caused a lot of stress and some hurt feelings."

"She's right," Sam cut in. "There were times when the tension was thick enough to cut. But I have to tell you a funny story, and it's true. When our fifth child was born at one o'clock in the morning, the nurse came out and said, 'Mr. Golden, you have a son.' Now, I had to try that on for size: *Five* sons. Five *sons*. FIVE SONS! No matter how I said it as I walked the hall, it came out with a beautiful sound. About a half-hour later they wheeled Evelyn out. She was in a daze—kind of semiconscious—and when I walked up and took her hand, she was muttering, 'Five daughters-in-law. Oy vey, *five* daughters-in-law.' Can you believe it; she was already uptight about daughters-in-law, and the oldest boy was only ten."

Scene 2—Morris and Kay

Few towns and cities seem to measure up to their image, but without question, Muncie, Indiana, *is* "Middletown, U.S.A." The narrow streets are lined with sensible homes with a midwestern architectural look—most of them squatting solidly under a canopy of trees.

Morris and Kay Easterley live in an unpretentious, two-story frame house out near the university. They, too, fit the Muncie image—dependable but not dull, a deep religious faith, comfortable with each other after thirty-one years of marriage, in good relationship now with their two daughters, both of whom live with their families in Indianapolis.

Had the children put a strain on their marriage during the early years?

Kay was thoughtful for a minute or so and then said, "My relationship with our oldest daughter developed into a heavy strain. She was a very strong-willed child. We seemed to clash often, and I felt she deliberately defied me. There was a lot of hostility between us which created tension and stress. There were times, I know, when I was hard to live with, but usually Morris and I could talk it out, and he helped me hold on with a little objectivity. He tried to help me see that I was pushing Phyllis too hard. I've been told I'm a perfectionist, and my expectations were probably too high. She and I have had several discussions about that time of our lives since Phyllis has become an adult, and one day she said something that really shook me: 'It was wonderful to have you for a mother, but it was hard to be your daughter.'"

We sat quietly for a while reflecting on that comment, and then Morris said, "Yes, there were times when the children were in the way. I would want to take Kay out alone so just the two of us could be together, but she wouldn't leave the girls. This made me feel that she put the children ahead of me. I felt hurt about that, and there were some tense scenes. We'd try to work through those times. Now and then we were successful, but once in a while we really got bogged down."

Scene 3—Willard and Jane

Responding to the same question, Jane Henry said, "Yes, the children put stress on our marriage. We didn't have enough time together before the children started to arrive. When they were small, we would try to get away now and then for a weekend, but we couldn't afford it very often. It was great, though, when we could, and it was important to our marriage. But it was frustrating with five kids in the house. There were times when I felt resentful about being tied down so close, and then I would feel guilty for reacting that way. This made for some pretty unpleasant times."

Willard Henry's reactions were not the least bit uncommon among the men we talked with: "So much time and effort was devoted to the kids that I felt like a stranger around here. And at times like that it was pretty easy to get to feeling sorry for myself. Then I would sulk; this was my way of letting her know that something was wrong, and we'd better get with it."

And Inez Schwartz, whose divorce became final just eight months before we talked, was still feeling raw after living through the breakup of her marriage of twenty years. "I think having children is a rewarding experience, but we didn't have enough time to secure our relationship before they came. Because of the makeup of our two personalities it might not have made any difference, but I've often wondered whether if we had waited it might not have worked out better. There's no doubt that it put a big strain on our relationship."

A Drastic Turning Point

Dr. Robert Blood helps us better understand these reactions with his comment that while the changes brought on by the arrival of a baby in the home may not necessarily be resented, "they are more drastic than at any other turning point in life, not excluding marriage."[3] There's no doubt that when two become three, most couples feel the excitement and joy of creation. But the change is forever. Dr. Blood continues:

> A baby inevitably alters the husband-wife relationship. Where before the two could focus on each other, now there is a distraction. Or perhaps it should be called an attraction. Both parents' attention is diverted to the child. His needs and interests compete with those of the partner. As more children arrive, each family member's slice of attention gets thinner.[4]

Harriett and I have vivid recollections of experiencing stress between us when our daughter was small. The entry of a baby into our home after two years of marriage created intense excitement, but at the same time it completely revolutionized our lifestyle. Nothing was or could be the same again. Our attention was focused on that new little person in the crib—the result of our lovemaking. It was awesome except when the diapers needed changing, or it was time for the two o'clock in the morning feeding, or when I got that "I'm too tired" look and sigh in response to my not-so-subtle advances.

But then, great are the rewards of watching the baby grow and develop as the months move through the first year and then on to the second birthday! And great is the opportunity for the stress of those months to erupt into distress as feelings of weariness and neglect and displacement weigh heavily on a couple struggling to understand and cope with a wholly new relationship. The tendency during this time is to concentrate so much time and attention on the child that the parents often neglect each other.

With perceptive insight Evelyn Duvall explains:

> While the baby is learning what it means to become a human being by growing, developing, and achieving his developmental tasks, his mother is learning how to be a mother, his father is practicing what it means to be a father, and the new family is settling itself into family patterns for the first time in history. This involves the simultaneous working out of the developmental tasks of the baby, the mother, the father, and the family as a whole.[5]

An aware couple will come to recognize this triangular struggle for identity as an opportunity for growth. Commitment to each other and to the family will generally hold them steady during the periods of strain. Expressions of love for each other, spoken and acted out, will tend to keep stressful moments from exploding into distressful and angry scenes, which not only are injurious to the marriage relationship but telegraph hurtful messages of rejection to the baby.

A Critical Time to Cultivate the Relationship

During the ten to twelve years that follow the birth of the first child, the marriage relationship itself must be cultivated consciously. This requires dedication and thought. The situation is compounded by the fact that it is during these years parents and children alike are trying hard to grow and develop in their respective roles—roles for which no one is adequately prepared.

Pollster George Gallup, Jr., recognized this weakness when he said, "One key reason for the threatened dissolution of the family unit is that while rearing children is our most vital role in life, we seem to be least prepared for this role. We plunge into marriage and raise children without any advance knowledge and learn our way by trial and error."[6] Psychologist Richard Farson adds both light and heat to the complex task facing parents: "Anyone who isn't bewildered by child-rearing and doesn't find it an extremely formidable and trying experience probably isn't a parent."[7]

Bewildering . . . formidable . . . trying. Most everyone we've talked with agrees, as attested to by these random comments from our interviews:

"I think having children is a rewarding experience, but there is no doubt it puts a big strain on the relationship."

"I would say there never was a time when I wished we didn't have kids, but there were times when the children caused stress between us."

"Maybe we wouldn't have the problems we have today it we hadn't had our third child. I think that was a major disaster."

"Frank felt the strain. I did not. I felt very comfortable and happy raising the kids."

The temptation is strong to let the marriage take a back seat to the children as parents struggle with the complexities of child-rearing. And yet, while every early learning experience a child has is vital to his or her development as a person, *we believe that the awareness of a deep, expressive, and passionate love between the mother and father is the base upon which everything else is built.* Our friend and colleague Charlie Shedd says, "The best thing I can do for my children is to love their mother."

The Need for Agreement

The potential for stress and distress within the marriage brought on by the presence of one or more children in the home is usually multiplied many times over by the struggle for consensus between husband and wife on the whole idea of child-rearing. Debilitating distress over incompatible concepts of child-rearing and discipline can cause a breakdown in the marriage relationship.

Some form of agreement and mutual understanding about child-rearing is essential to a happy and balanced family life. Among the many things a couple will find helpful to discuss between themselves before starting a family are their individual ideas about this delicate and complex task. As a husband and wife share reactions to their own growing-up experience, they stand to gain a deeper understanding of the attitudes that are likely to shape their future marriage and family patterns. Much is to be gained by forging a pattern of family values out of awareness and sensitivity to each other's feelings and ideas.

It is grossly naive of any couple to assume it is possible to just stumble into a healthy family pattern in which the day-to-day stresses are handled well. Evelyn Duvall writes:

> Democratic child-rearing is not anything that comes "naturally." It requires a firm set of family values and a willingness to pursue them diligently. It protects the

rights of each member of the family, regardless of age or sex. It shares responsibility with all family members according to their capacities. It fosters neither laissez-faire anarchy nor unrestricted license, but values rather self-disciplined, goal-directed individuals. It demands the courage for verbal and non-verbal communication, openness and responsiveness with others, and the ability to handle abstractions as well as concrete things and thoughts. It thrives best within a relatively favorable climate where the struggle for survival is not ever-present.[8]

Actions Speak Loudest

The sensitive and caring parent, keenly aware of the stresses both inside and outside the home which press heavily on the growing child, constantly attempts to adapt and guide without overreacting. But the people we've talked with as we have attempted to find clues to lasting marriage and a happy family life, readily agree that their development was affected far more *by the attitudes and actions of their parents—positively and negatively—than by anything that was told them.* It is generally agreed that a mother and father are the most significant role models a boy or girl will ever have—an intensely sobering thought for any parent!

This truth rolled over Harriett like a flood one day as she was interviewing forty-three-year-old Ilka Wilson. Her marriage had collapsed two years before when her husband left and moved in with another woman. This was a shattering blow to their three children, but especially to Faye, their oldest daughter, because she had been so close to her father.

Ilka's deep feelings of bitterness and hurt could be clearly heard: "Faye was about seventeen at the time, and one night a few days after her daddy left, she stayed out all night. I was frantic but decided not to call the police. Finally, she came in about eight o'clock in the morning. I met her at the door, and asked, 'Faye, have you been with that boy all night long?' Her response broke my heart: 'Yes, if Dad can go out and do this, I can too.'

"When her father heard what she had done, he was furious and confronted her with it. She looked him right in the eye and said, 'I'm not hurting anyone else by what I'm doing, but look at the people you've hurt.' Would you believe? He didn't see any connection between what he had done and Faye's behavior. He just said, 'That is different.' "

But for Faye it wasn't different. While children are well aware that their parents are human beings, they look to them as models of what life is all about. If parental attitudes and behavior are excessively rigid and puritanical, the chances are strong that this will carry into their own marriage and family relationship. On the other hand, if the example given is one in which love and affirmation are freely expressed physically and verbally and in which guidelines and standards are clear, it is likely this will set the style for the children's attitudes and actions later.

Children tend to internalize the strengths and weaknesses of their parents' family style and then reproduce these same attitudes and actions in their own marriage and family relationships. The good news is, though, that a negative cycle can be broken by a keen awareness of what is happening and by exerting conscious effort to build a positive pattern of relationships. Change is possible!

The following quotation by Dorothy Law Nolte has been widely circulated in several forms. We believe its implications for every parent—and grandparent—are profound:

A child that lives with ridicule learns to be timid.
A child that lives with criticism learns to condemn.
A child that lives with distrust learns to be deceitful.
A child that lives with antagonism learns to be hostile.
A child that lives with affection learns to love.
A child that lives with encouragement learns
   confidence.
A child that lives with truth learns justice.
A child that lives with praise learns to appreciate.
A child that lives with sharing learns to be
   considerate.
A child that lives with knowledge learns wisdom.
A child that lives with patience learns to be tolerant.
A child that lives with happiness will find love and
   beauty.

Reactions about Discipline

The reactions from virtually all of the people we interviewed seem to indicate that one of the major causes of marital stress is the partners' differing ideas about how to discipline their children. Ruth, a mother of four, volunteered, "We were in disagreement about discipline of the children. I was terribly lax. I was always trying to do things with psychology, and Ed had a yes or no answer for everything. I thought he was too strict, so we had sharp differences about discipline. This created a lot of tension between us. And our children were aware of this and took advantage of it."

Scene 4—Viola and Bill
Viola, whose husband travels for a national food company and is gone Monday through Friday every week, recalled, "Much of the time we didn't agree on how to go about

disciplining the children. It was hard for Bill after being gone all week to arrive home on Friday and fall right into the rhythm of the home. Sometimes when he would walk in things seemed serene and peaceful on the surface, but it had really been an awful week, and he just couldn't understand why I was uptight. Then when I would tell him about some of the troubles I'd had with the kids, they seemed trivial compared to the competitive battles he had been fighting all week. All of this added up to tension and stress between us.

"But we were aware most of the time of what was happening to us and worked hard at our relationship. Both of us believed that our marriage was important. We wanted to be good parents. But we also knew the time would come when the kids would be gone and there would be just the two of us left at home. So, we tried constantly to find ways to come together and resolve our differences and make things work." Viola stopped and looked over at Bill with an amazed expression on her face, and said, "Golly, honey, that was quite a speech. I don't think I've ever expressed my feelings quite this way before. How do you feel about it?"

With an amused expression on his face, Bill responded, "I think you described it pretty well. Those were rough times, and your ideas about raising the children and how they should be disciplined were usually quite different from mine. We don't even see eye to eye now on how our kids are handling their children. But I think the thing that saved us was that we did talk about it and worked out compromises between us. And we always tried to let the kids know that we loved them and they were important to us. Sure, there are things I'd do differently today, but I guess what we did wasn't too far wrong because we have a good relationship with the children now. We respect them, and they seem to feel the same way about us."

Discipline versus Punishment

It is not our purpose here to prescribe a preferred pattern of discipline or to affirm any of the several approaches that show up in books and lectures. But we do suggest the importance of a couple working together to hammer out a correction and discipline style compatible to their mutual feelings. And we'll only slant these comments enough to urge recognition of the difference between "discipline" and "punishment."

There are some significant findings by competent researchers which suggest that, as a rule, punishment is not a deterrent to future misbehavior. Rather, it tends to humiliate and frequently causes a deep and crippling resentment that may color behavior and relationships for a lifetime. I can't help wondering about the future of a little boy whose mother or father is swatting away angrily on his behind all the way down the aisle of the grocery story. The flailing hand, contorted face, and shrill tone of voice broadcast to the child and anyone within hearing distance that whatever the child has done has produced an angry parent, who apparently cares little at this point about anyone's feelings. Why should it come as a surprise to anyone if that child grows up to be physically and verbally aggressive and abusive?

The Stressful Teen Years

In reflecting on all that we have heard about child stress on the marriage relationship, Harriett concludes: "I can see why husbands feel the tension and I can remember feeling it myself. It seemed like there were times when I was so physically and emotionally drained that I had nothing left of myself to give Floyd. And I think that weathering the teenage years is just as difficult, if not more so, than any other time. These can be very stressful years for a married couple.

"It is hard to begin the process of letting them go, of turning them loose to become persons in their own right. Coping with the girlfriends and boyfriends, dating, and pressures for a car, are just a few of the universal concerns that create stress. This was perhaps the most difficult time for me."

In one way or another, the feelings Harriett has expressed were repeated again and again by virtually everyone we have talked with. By the time a couple has been married twelve to eighteen years, they are struggling with their own relationship and feelings toward each other. The husband is submerged in the struggle to make good in his work or profession—an all-consuming task in the complex and competitive milieu of these closing years of the twentieth century. And the trauma of unfulfilled dreams has scarred his thinking.

It is at this time, too, that the wife who has worked at a job outside the home or full-time within the home may become painfully aware of the haunting specter of middle age. Along with that comes the paralyzing fear that she may not be as sexually attractive to her husband as she once was.

This is heavy baggage for a couple to carry at the same time their teenage children are wrestling with the pain of growing up and are struggling for independence. An awareness that all members of the family are involved in common growth experiences may well open the door for an empathetic understanding which can ease the burden for everyone.

Scene 5—Rex and Jan

Rex and Jan Lowell are a typical middle-class couple who made their way through the first twenty-two years of marriage with nothing more than the usual problems common to most of us. Then their middle son, a university student, got involved in the drug scene. "We went through two years of pure hell with him," Jan remembered. "While the hurt and anxiety were excruciating, there was just no end to the patience Rex had with him. His dad never gave up or threatened to kick him out. He finally dropped out of school, but we stood by and loved him. It wasn't easy, but somehow we managed with God's help to hold steady."

Rex and Jan plotted a course which prevented the stress of those years from exploding into distress, and together they helped their son through his problem and on to the completion of his education. For us, Rex and Jan epitomize a statement that Peter de Vries made: "The value of marriage is not that adults produce children, but that children produce adults."

How does Jan feel as she looks back on those days and reflects on the lessons learned? "It's the crises in life that help us grow as persons, spiritually and in every other way. Only a very shallow person never has any mountains to climb or any crises to cope with. Material things are not as important to us as they once were. Every day is a special gift because we don't know about tomorrow, but we are thankful for our blessings."

What Happened to Privacy?

It is during the years when teenagers are in the home that sexual stress often threatens to inflame the marriage relationship. There is the danger, of course, that familiarity can lead to staleness. The single-eyed involvement of a husband caught in the make-good rat race may take the edge off of sexual excitement. And the "be all things to all members of the family" syndrome—doing the shopping, maintaining the home, being a super-mother and supportive wife, active in P.T.A. and church and community projects—can easily drain off all desire for sex. All of these factors impose severe strain on a couple's ability to function happily and satisfactorily in the bedroom. But added to these pressures is the frustrating problem of lack of privacy.

This was aired quite candidly by a member of the Phil Donahue show audience one day when a woman asked a marriage counselor guest: "What do you do when you have teenagers in the home who know what is going on when you and your husband go back to the bedroom and lock the door?" Good question! The marriage counselor admitted this was a situation that every married couple with teenagers in the home would have to face. He didn't give any flip answers, but emphasized the importance of recognizing the problem for what it is and taking definite steps to respond to it.

Frank Gomez had obviously thought a lot about this question and tells his young married friends "that if they think they have problems now, just wait until their kids are teenagers. The physical side of marriage practically dissolves then. There's plenty of stress, and you just have to work at it and be patient with one another until you get past that stage."

Another couple, Ken and Velma, solved it this way. When their children reached the ages of eight, nine, and thirteen, they held a family conference one night. Ken opened the discussion: "As we all get older, times of privacy are just as important to each of us as the times when we're all together. It is important for you, and for your mother and me. Now, here's what I think we ought to do. I'm going to have locks put on all of our bedroom doors. When any of us feel the need to be alone for any reason, we can go to our rooms and lock the door. We'll respect your closed doors, and we hope you'll treat us the same way. One thing we all need to agree on, though: none of us will ever knock on someone's door unless there is a real emergency—remember, a *real* emergency."

Did it work? "You just wouldn't believe how well it worked," Velma responded. "The kids thought that was a neat idea. And you know what? Only once during all the years that the kids were at home was there a knock on our bedroom door, and that was one Sunday afternoon when our youngest broke his arm falling out of a tree. And we honored the rules with them too."

In talking with us about sexual pressures Sue and Fred had when their children were teenagers, Sue related: "Fred and I have always had a good sexual relationship. And I think most of the time we just went to bed and locked the door without giving it a second thought. I remember one night when two of the girls were having a boyfriend crisis and were sprawling and bawling all over the house. Fred and I finally retreated to the patio, but we couldn't shut out the commotion. I'd had it! After a while Fred looked over at me and said, 'Let's forget this mess and go catch worms in one of those old bottles.' We did just that; we found in each other the love and warmth and intimacy that comes from such times. This doesn't mean that we loved our children less. But one reason we've had such a good marriage is that our sex life has always been important to us. And I think this has made us better parents."

Beverly expressed another point of view: "I think married sex is like seasons. You don't always have the same amount of stuff going for you, but then again, there are times when you do. During the time when our kids were growing up, we were having business and money problems. There was just a lot of junk going on that threw us out of step sexually. But we realized that was all part of the change and growth process. We've always been friends first of all, and I think that is why our marriage has been able to take a lot of stuff; the basic commitment was there. We weren't relying totally on sex as a basis for our relationship at that time."

The Positive Side

The stresses on a couple's marriage relationship are as many and varied as there are people. There is every indication that the traumas which begin with the birth of the first child and continue through each stage of child-rearing register high on a married couple's seismograph. And the aftershocks seem to continue with regularity until the last child leaves home. On this there is almost universal agreement.

But in our research and conversations we also found general agreement by persons, still married or divorced, as to the deep joy and personal satisfaction derived from their children. And while the Census Bureau statistics document dramatic changes in family life patterns, George Gallup, Jr., in a 1979 speech, said, "Three out of four women in the United States say marriage and children are among the most important of the elements that provide satisfaction for them."

According to Dr. Norval Glenn, more than 90 percent of the respondents to a 1989 family values study said that a happy marriage was most important to them, and more than one-third chose a traditional marriage in which the husband is the breadwinner and the wife a homemaker.[9]

We find this encouraging. The changes that have rocked and shocked our culture in the last forty years stagger the imagination. These have inevitably affected attitudes and directions of marriage and family life. But we do not believe a doomsday attitude is the answer, nor does it jibe with most of what we hear and read. We dare not fall into the trap of labeling every facet of change as a sure step toward moral decay and the disintegration of healthy marriage and family life.

At the same time, a married couple cannot remain oblivious to the stresses that could explode into distress and rock the relationship—especially those related to the presence of children in the home. An awareness of what can and is happening seems vital if a couple is to avoid the irrational overcompensation and overreacting that cause turbulence within the family.

The Big Questions and Possible Solutions

Now to the big questions:

- How can a married couple creatively handle the stresses caused by the presence of children in the home?
- What can a married couple do that will work in their favor to prevent parent-child relationships from becoming distressful and crippling to their marriage?

Obviously, these are major questions; and while we may not offer comprehensive answers, we do want to share the specific feelings, attitudes, and reactions that have emerged from our hundreds of hours of conversation and from our own experience.

1. *Maintain a daily awareness that for your marriage to be healthy you must pay attention to each other.* Awareness of a problem or a potential problem is usually the first step

toward its solution. Dr. Charles Figley, a research psychologist and marriage counselor at Purdue University, agrees that generally a couple's sense of satisfaction in marriage drops during the child-rearing years. One reason for this, he suggests, is that "marriage takes a back seat to the children. We're constantly being told that we have to tell our children every day how much we love them, and that's good. And if you're not doing something with your children, you feel guilty. But you only have so much time, so something's got to give, and the marriage goes first."[10]

No matter how long a couple has been together, the marriage relationship has little chance of remaining healthy and vital if it takes a back seat to anything. If it is tops in priority, every other relationship in life will be enriched.

2. *In an atmosphere of verbal and nonverbal warmth, maintain clearly understood guidelines for behavior and discipline which respect the integrity and personhood of the husband, wife, and children.* It is grossly unrealistic for a married couple to think they can devise a plan that will eliminate times of conflict with their children and in so doing avoid stress in their own relationship. However, the wise and aware couple will direct their energies and creative abilities toward establishing and maintaining a plan of child-rearing and a climate in the home that is conducive to the physical, emotional, and spiritual growth of the child. At the same time parents will supply their children with the resources to react in a mature and grown-up way during the inevitable periods of stress.

Dr. Dian Baumrind of the University of California describes this kind of affirming environment in which "the child is directed firmly, consistently, and rationally; issues rather than personalities are focused upon; parent uses power when necessary; parent values obedience to adult requirements, as well as independence in the child; parent sets standards and enforces them firmly but does not regard self as infallible; parent listens to child but does not base decisions solely on child's desires.... Most important, keep listening and take into consideration what your child has to tell you."[11]

A rather significant reaction seemed to emerge in our conversation with people: Those who had been raised within a rigid, authoritarian system, where there was little or no physical and verbal warmth between husband and wife and parents and children, testified to an explosive and unpleasant or dehumanizing atmosphere of indifference. On the other hand, where an aura of warmth and affection and spiritual sensitivity was characteristic of the husband-wife-child relationship, those inevitable periods of marriage and family stress had in most cases been worked through in a nonexplosive and reasonable way. In other words, when there existed verbal and nonverbal warmth, combined with firm disciplinary standards and clear guidelines for behavior, the potential for distress between child and parents and between husband and wife was minimized.

3. *Acceptance and the giving of unconditional love seem to offer a setting within which each family member can grow and develop.* There is a wide agreement among child psychologists and psychiatrists that a distressful climate can better be avoided where love is expressed, verbally and nonverbally, without conditions for behavior being imposed. The "I will love you if . . ." statement or attitude is almost certain to produce resentment and create distressful scenes.

Harriett and I watched a scene a few years ago that illustrates the power of unconditional love. A family was seated near us at a restaurant—a mother, dad, a boy of about eight, and a dark, curly-headed, bright-eyed little fellow of about five. David, the five-year-old, wormed and squirmed all over his chair and at one point even made it under the table. He kept up a running monologue, punctuated now and then with a question directed at his mother and father, who were trying to read the morning paper. We were both amazed at the easy give-and-take that was going on in spite of David's perpetual motion and running conversation. Suddenly, David looked over at his father and asked, "Daddy, do you love me when I'm bad?" Looking up from his paper, Dad responded, "Of course I do, David. When you're bad, it makes me mad, but I still love you."

The scene at the table radiated love and acceptance. The smile on David's face indicated his satisfaction with both the words and his dad's tone of voice. Truly unconditional love between husband and wife and between parents and children may seem impossible from a human point of view, but it is a worthy goal to strive for.

4. *Learn that apron strings can strangle the children and a marriage. Release brings growth and enrichment.* Someone has said, "There are only two lasting bequests we can hope to give our children. One of these is roots; the other, wings." While the giving of wings is an essential part of each stage of child development and family life, a married couple usually feels this stress most acutely during the teenage or launching years. These are crucial times of adjustment and change. The balance between letting go and maintaining order and respect is precarious, and the balance between doing too much and not doing enough is often agonizing. And yet there's a lot of truth in a statement Dr. Haim Ginott made somewhere, "The measure of a good parent is in what he is willing *not* to do for his child."

The letting-go process can create enormous pressures between a husband and wife. For, as Dr. Henri Nouwen writes, "The difficult task of parenthood is to help children grow to the freedom that permits them to stand on their own two feet, physically, mentally, and spiritually, and to allow them to move away in their own direction."[12]

And a book that was invaluable to Harriett and me in our own growth experience as a couple and as parents stated:

> In our most humble and sincere efforts to restrict and confine our children and to tighten the tourniquet of social inhibitions, we undoubtedly trace the pattern of many future tragedies. It is the unfortunate result of attempting to enforce too many rules—of struggling too hard to make children "good," and striving too little to make them happy and contented. It may be beautifully poetic to speak of children as "bits of human clay to be molded." But it is very poor psychology. Children are little bits of living protoplasm, who need merely to be guided.[13]

Wise words, we believe, as a couple struggles to maintain a constant awareness that happiness and success in the marriage and family relationship are more likely to come as we attempt to lovingly guide our children into growth experiences, and release them to learn their own lessons when the time is right.

Chapter Nine

The Twin Stresses of Money and Work

*Family discord is frequently attributable to a
failure to agree on how to spend money. . . .
Approximately one couple in five had never
satisfactorily agreed upon finances, although the
couples had been married an average of twenty
years.*   Judson T. and Mary G. Landis

*Without question, a major reason for the rising
divorce rate in this country is the long hours spent
on the job.*   Ted W. Engstrom and David J. Juroe

There is widespread agreement among authorities on marriage that Americans fight more over money than any other single area of conflict.

This is borne out graphically by a study conducted by John and Letha Scanzoni in 1975 in which 3,096 husbands and wives were interviewed, and "33 percent reported money matters as the major area of marital disagreement." Child-related matters ran second with 19 percent.[1] And responses to the money-related questions in our research interviews underscore with almost frightening intensity the Scanzoni percentages. Money—how to get it, how to spend it—is a major stress point in marriage and family life today.

Scene 1—Della

Della Hansen, a cool, self-assured, outgoing woman of forty-six, had been divorced just sixteen months when we spent an afternoon in her north Seattle home. In spite of the trauma of divorce after twenty and one-half years of marriage, she seemed to have her act pretty well together.

Two affairs—that she knew about—had wrecked her marriage. The last one drove her to divorce—a divorce her husband didn't want. But neither did he understand Della's unwillingness to continue their marriage while he kept the other woman: "He liked the idea of marriage, wife, and children; that was a good front, but he wanted romance on the outside. Can you believe it? He really asked if I'd put up with him having a mistress!"

But when we talked about the things that drove a wedge into their relationship throughout all the years of their marriage, Della responded, "Money was the big problem, and next in line that made me unhappy was his working all the time.

"I worked in the bank before we were married, so it was quite natural for me to handle the finances. But we hadn't been married long before all that changed. We had a big blow-up one night because Ken wanted to go out with a couple of his friends, and I didn't have enough cash in the house to take care of what he thought he'd need. That night he took the finances out of my hands, and from then on all I got was an allowance to run the household.

"But even though Ken had a good job there was never enough money to go around. The front we put up was very important to him. He bought expensive clothes for himself, for me, and for the children. We had two homes and drove big cars; we skied a lot, and all five of us had the finest ski equipment money could buy. But Ken didn't like to settle down and pay the bills, so he would let them go for five or six months at a time. I remember one time when the fuel company wouldn't deliver the heating oil because the last bill hadn't been paid.

"I guess Ken always wanted to put on a good show but wasn't willing to pay the price for it. This left all of us in hot water. I was embarrassed and worried most of the time. The pressure would build up and then we'd have a big explosion. Everything about our marriage seemed to turn sour, but I was scared and didn't think I could make it on my own, so I just held on and hoped for the best."

It seems fairly clear that Della and Ken Hansen brought widely conflicting views about money into their marriage. Their sense of values was miles apart and remained that way throughout the twenty years of their life together. Discord over money and its use moved through every part of their relationship like a spreading cancer, until there was nothing left to salvage.

And while it is true that Della and Ken's conflict and distress over money were probably more severe and disastrous than that of any other couple we talked with, the majority of couples recognized this to be a major area of stress in their marriages.

Scene 2—Lars and Linda

There was a tenseness about Lars and Linda Harvey that made us uneasy. Their home in south Houston was comfortable but not pretentious. Neither Lars nor Linda was the least bit reluctant to talk about the problems in their marriage. It was interesting, though, that when we asked Linda about the importance of a mutually satisfactory sex relationship to their marriage, she responded, "Oh, I think it is terribly important, but not nearly as important as agreement on finances. We have no problems sexually and never had. There's just no way our sex life could be improved as far as I'm concerned. But good sex won't solve any of the other problems. Lars and I couldn't be more sexually compatible, but we still have lots of problems and always have—especially over money."

When we turned to Lars for his response, he said, "She's right. I think our biggest problems have come from the financial side of our relationship. We started off in a hole, and we've been fighting an uphill battle ever since. Sure, we wouldn't have any financial problems if we decided to live in a smaller house and simplify our whole lifestyle, but we've never been ready to do that."

With that admission, the discussion shifted. What were their dreams for the future? Linda's words tumbled out in a tense and shrill tone: "To get settled in a place where I feel at home—and stay there. I wish my husband had time to play some golf and putter around the yard with me. I wish he had time to focus attention on me and the home rather than on his work."

What about Lar's dreams? "I'd like to have a job that would make it possible for me to do what she asks. But I can't do it in my present position, and yet I don't want to change jobs. There is just no way I can make enough money to get the material things we both seem to want."

Throughout their twenty-seven years of married life Lars' salary had never been enough, and their wants and values had always been at odds. While they had a lot going for them in other ways, disagreement about money boiled over and chipped away at their relationship.

Who Holds the Purse Strings?

Mike and Jane Davis had a breezy but an apparently solid relationship. When it came to money, Jane said, "He makes the money, and I spend it. Sure it creates tension and stress—nothing big, you understand, but it's always there. I like to write checks but can never keep my checkbook straight. I'm not a good money manager. To me, money brings all kinds of pleasures, and I just love to spend it."

But Mike and Jane had come to understand their differences in money values, and they could talk about it. Mike said, "Look, I love Jane, and we've had a happy twenty-three years. Sure we get uptight about the way Jane handles money, but we try to check signals once a week to make sure she hasn't gone overboard. Years ago we talked about this, and she agreed to put up with what she thought were my conservative and narrow ideas about money, and I agreed to try to understand what I thought were her wild ideas. Because of our commitment to each other, we work at it constantly—and talk about it. That way there aren't any explosions and harsh words."

Sally and Maurice Johnson both worked, and between the two of them they were making about $35,000 a year. Sally surprised us a little by saying, "Maurice and I agree on money matters most of the time. I handle the money because that's the way he wants it. It is hard to make it go around, but our home is comfortable and the children have what they need, even though they may not be the best dressed kids on the block."

Maurice shrugged his shoulders and said, "It's *our* money, not mine or hers. She knows how much we've got and how to handle it. I'd rather she did it—my masculinity is not dependent on whether I hold the purse strings or not. Anyway, I read somewhere that about 80 percent of the money spent by American families is handled by women. So I guess that puts us with the majority."

Accepting Your Differences

"Values differ between husbands and wives as well as between families. When they do, the usual processes of decision-making and conflict-resolution come into play."[2]

The fact that we bring differing sets of money values into marriage should come as no surprise to any of us. For diversity makes the difference between people and robots—and who wants to be married to a robot?

It is important, however, for a couple *to accept the reality of their differences and, when they surface, to discuss them openly with each other and arrive at mutually acceptable solutions*. We cannot overemphasize the necessity of talking things over in the sensitive area of money handling and management, where differences of attitude so frequently occur.

It seems to us that a greater surprise would be for a husband and wife to have identical ideas and attitudes on how to spend money. Each of us carries our own money baggage into our relationships, and even if our backgrounds are similar, we are likely to react differently to them. This has been true of Harriett and me. The frugality of a Methodist parsonage during my teenage years in the 1930s closely matched the experiences Harriett had as the daughter of a worker in the California oil fields. Consequently, we both carried ultraconservative feelings about money into our marriage. But as the years have passed, Harriett has done a better job of shaking loose from those restrictive feelings than I have. I still find it unpleasant to buy a new suit—probably a negative carryover from the memory of graduating from high school in a borrowed dark blue suit. And it is always downright painful for me to buy a new car (with the exception of that red convertible!). In fact, I can be sure of losing at least one night's sleep after the purchase papers have been signed.

And while there have been and still are plenty of areas of conflict between us, the spending of money has not created distressful explosions in our relationship. We're not sure just why this is, except that we have usually been able to discuss our conflicting attitudes. In this part of our lives we've come to a good understanding and appreciation of the other's feelings. Consequently, most of the time each of us has managed to react reasonably well when the other has overspent or underspent or spent foolishly.

From our discussions with the many people who have shared thoughts on their marriage relationship with us, we've come to feel that the creative handling of money stress, as with other stresses, begins with a recognition and acceptance of our differences and the reasons for them. This awareness can then lead to respect for each other's personhood, an appreciation for the other's point of view whether we agree with it or not, and a recognition of the idea that seldom does anyone set out deliberately to do a stupid thing or make a bad decision. And in this kind of climate there is less room for bitter recrimination or blame.

Scene 3—Alex and Vivian

But, of course, none of us are 100 percenters when it comes to doing what we know to do. This was vividly illustrated in our conversation with Alex and Vivian Collins. Alex opened with a complaint that obviously had brought considerable heat to their relationship:

"One thing which really burns me up is that Vivian never seems to have confidence in my business and investment decisions. Right now I've got a real estate deal going that I thought was a good one. She wasn't very enthusiastic about it, and that didn't help my confidence any because I admit I don't know much about real estate. Anyway, a couple of nights ago I was sound asleep when Vivian came into the bedroom and woke me up with, 'Now I know why you were able to buy that land so cheap. I just heard over the television news that the odor is so bad out there no one can stand it.' She woke me up out of a sound sleep to give me the business about what she thought was a bad deal. That really irritated me!

"So I make some bad investments once in a while! I know I'm impatient and don't always investigate things the way I should. But now and then I make some good investments. Just last week I came in and told her I had made three thousand dollars on the stock market. You know what she said? 'How about that loser you had last week?' At times like that I just want to go off and forget her for awhile."

All of this sounds a little harsh and angry on paper, but there was no escaping the comfortable rapport that seemed to exist between them. Vivian spoke up: "There is another place where I get in his hair. He always feels that I do too much for the children."

"That's right," Alex cut in. "And I've talked with her about that. I think our kids ought to make their own way just like we did. Sure, once in a while Vivian's parents would slip us a hundred dollars, and when that happened we felt rich. Now we give our kids a thousand dollars and they just act like they deserve it. It's not that I'm tight or don't love them; I just don't think it is good for them."

It was obvious that money was a stress point between Alex and Vivian, but it was also pretty obvious that they could talk about it—and even joke about it. This was their way of working through differences and preventing explosive scenes which could then spread to painful and crippling distress.

Working It Out

Now, we're not ready to make any "God Almighty" statements about how every couple should handle their money or how they should resolve problems when they come up. We do know what has worked for us (and I suppose we think at times that what has worked for us should work for anybody!). Since we happen to believe in an equalitarian marriage style, this carries over into our financial affairs. I have always felt that any major expenditure of money—cars, furnishings, donations to church or charitable organizations, gadgets, whatever—should be agreed upon mutually. We usually discuss the minor expenditures as well, and if we don't agree, we don't spend.

Sure, there have been times when each of us was upset because the other didn't see things our way. And occasionally one of us will move to a different viewpoint after thinking a matter through more carefully. But for us, at least, we feel strongly that unilateral decisions aren't good. When it comes to money or anything else, our long-term partnership calls for talking about it and then agreeing on the action we'll take. And that isn't always easy.

The nitty-gritty of *how* a couple handles their money—the making of budgets, the manipulation of credit cards, details on how to save, agreeing on when and how to make a major purchase—should be left to other discussions. Many good books and papers written by experts are devoted to this subject and are readily available to any inquiring couple. Excellent counsel can also be obtained from your banker or a local financial advisor, who is equipped to suggest possible solutions in keeping with your specific circumstances.

But our findings seem to indicate that a key to avoiding bitter marital disagreement over money stress is the constant recognition that very natural and honest differences exist. And from there a couple can forge a pattern of open communication which, while disagreements will occur, will open the possibility for negotiation and resolution. Economist Paula Nelson commented in an interview, "Money has taken the place of sex—at least, in conversations. The most intelligent thing a married couple can do is sit down and write questions and their goals. That's where they start talking and facing reality."[3] Unlike many problems, though, it isn't likely this one will ever be resolved permanently. It requires two people working at it every day.

Consumed by Work

You recall that while Della Hansen said money was the big problem in her marriage, next in line was her husband's "working all the time." And Linda Harvey said, "I wish my husband had time to . . . putter around the yard with me. I wish he had time to focus attention on me and the house rather than his work." And now with many women also working long hours in chosen careers, time together can be hard to come by.

The irrepressible drive to make good at one's job or profession is certainly another major contributor to stress in today's society. This pressure seems to hold true as young men and women struggle to make their way up the business or corporate ladder and continues as they struggle to maintain their positions later in the middle years. We've heard these fears and pressures expressed throughout a cross-section of society—from small, independent businessmen to professionals in law and medicine to classroom teachers and administrators.

Perhaps nowhere is the potential for stress and distress within the work setting a greater hazard than in today's typical corporate structure. The potential dangers are pretty much the same whether the corporation is relatively small or whether it is a crawling complex of companies comprising a vast business empire. Men and women on each rung of the ladder find themselves lost and faceless—unsure of how to cope and have meaning in a new world dominated by puzzling and impersonal technology.

Psychiatrist Viktor Frankl views this setting and diagnoses this spreading malady as "executive disease," the symptoms of which are a scramble for power and attention.

And behind this scramble is the scream for recognition which tears at our deepest feelings. In a personal conversation several years ago in San Diego, Dr. Frankl repeated this theme, asserting that the pervasive illness that eats at the consciousness of people today is marked by feelings of alienation and aloneness—a loss of meaning. And perhaps nowhere is this attack felt more keenly than in our crowded and cacophonous urban centers.

But as we've thought about the so-called executive disease, our findings seem to indicate that it infects almost every area of our work life. It motivates our irrational need to succeed by society's standards. And in our search for meaning and for self-worth, it drives us relentlessly to a pathological devotion to the job, no matter how many hours are consumed, or whether our marriages and families suffer in the process.

We Are What We Do

I am always more than a little irritated when I meet people in a social situation, and the seemingly inevitable "What do you do?" question pops out early in the conversation. This comes across to me as if interest or acceptance is based on what you *do* rather than who you *are*. And I think we all struggle with this dehumanizing tendency to identify ourselves and others by our work. So often we do not value John and Jane Doe as persons, but rather see John Doe as an attorney or Jane Doe as a writer. This shallow and superficial pattern is recognized by Daniel Levinson when he writes, "A man's work is the primary base for his life in society. Through it he is 'plugged into' an occupational structure and a cultural, class and social matrix. Work is also of great sociological importance; it is a vehicle for the fulfillment or negation of central aspects of the self."[4]

Both Harriett and I want to be accepted and liked as *persons*—persons who are experiencing the roller coaster lows of failure, disappointment, frustration, and highs of love, happiness, and achievement. What we do shouldn't be important in our value to each other; it's who we are that counts. But unfortunately, for most people, work *is* the base for life in society. All too often our sense of self-worth is plugged into our daily work. And we have good reason to feel that our friends and associates value us in terms of what we do.

This distortion of human values puts an enormous strain on us. If we are valued by what we do and how well we do it, stifling pressure is exerted on us to succeed, to do better at our work than anyone else. We live in constant fear that if we don't measure up to the expectations of those in our social network, they may lose interest, and we can't handle the rejection.

Scene 4—Max and Reba

Max and Reba Hermann lived in a moderately comfortable home in one of the bedroom communities west of Chicago. Their third child had been married just five months before, and for the first time in twenty-five years, Max and Reba were alone. At ages forty-seven and forty-six they were struggling to find their way creatively into this new and unknown period in their relationship. As nearly as we could tell from our conversation, about the only cloud hanging over their life together was Max's apparent addiction to his work. He owned a furniture store in their town that evidently did quite well. Reba admitted that she had known from their earliest days together that Max was obsessed with his work. During the first years of their marriage the excuse was that they needed the money. But in later years this wasn't the case; although, as with most couples, they agreed that no matter how much they had, there always seemed to be a need for more.

Max spoke freely about the fact that personal achievement and the success of his business formed the base for his own feelings of self-worth. It was important to him for his friends, customers, and fellow townspeople to see him as a successful and affluent businessman. And he was willing to work twelve to fourteen hours a day to build and keep that image.

For the most part, Reba had managed to cope with her husband's neurotic addiction to his work so that their feelings of stress did not burst into angry and distressful scenes. But according to Reba, "About five years ago we really got embroiled in an ongoing family fight. The strain just got unbearable. Max felt that he should buy out the rest of the family interest in the furniture business. Most of the family wanted to sell, but there were some who didn't. They were convinced Max was trying to force them out and that I was pushing him to do it. Actually, I wasn't in favor of what Max wanted to do. But I was in the middle and the strain made me physically sick.

"Finally, one night I couldn't stand it any longer; so when Max got home from the store, I just made him get back in the car with me and we drove over to a lake about five miles out of town. We didn't talk much on the way home because I was upset and Max was mad at me for insisting that we go out before he had anything to eat.

"When we got parked, I said, 'We've got to talk about this whole mess; I can't take it any longer. Your family is trying to drive us apart, and I'm afraid they're going to succeed. How do I know you won't break under the pressure and just walk out? And I'm about to crack up, too. I'm scared.'

"Max just looked at me. His eyes were cold—there wasn't any sign of love in them at all. After a few moments of silence, he shouted, 'Look, our marriage contract is safe. No matter what happens we'll work things out. You haven't got anything to worry about.'

"While nothing was settled, and we weren't even able to touch each other, somehow I knew at that moment I was safe. If the marriage contract was secure, then there would be time to work things out. That crisis was the hardest thing we've ever had to face. It really got out of control for a while, but we both hung on by our fingernails until finally everything worked out."

While Max didn't make any further comment about his family crisis and what Reba had to say about his work habits, we could see from his attitude that he and Reba had found an accommodation for this stress-point in their lives. I especially like Harriett's reaction to our visit:

"While Floyd and I have never had the kind of family crisis Reba and Max experienced, I think Floyd has always had workaholic tendencies. I recall several times when we've had some very tense moments and conversations because I felt he was so buried in his work that nothing else seemed to matter. We have struggled with this in our relationship, and while I'm not ready to pronounce Floyd a completely recovered workaholic, we have in the past few years been able to discuss it and work at it without his becoming angry and resentful.

"For me, two things stand out in the Hermanns' story. First of all, I was really impressed with the scene in the car when Reba admitted she was about to crack up and was scared. Max's response told me, as it did Reba, that his commitment to their relationship was firm, and that even a crisis as traumatic as that one would not be allowed to fracture their marriage.

"I was also impressed with the fact that, even though it was obvious that work addiction was still a problem with Max, he and Reba had finally gotten it out in the open where they could talk about it. And in so doing they had been able to find a way to maintain their relationship. Talking it out opens the way to the healing of our fears and tensions."

Plague of the Workaholic

All too often the drive for social acceptance among our peers, along with the insatiable need to succeed, can so easily become a consuming passion. It seems anything short of acceptance and success robs us of our self-esteem. What was at one time a healthy and admirable motive to be at our best has now gotten out of control. When this happens, the trapped worker or harried professional becomes hopelessly entangled in a web of ten-, twelve-, or fifteen-hour workdays that strain physical and emotional energy to the breaking point.

The husband and wife who find themselves caught in this stressful milieu have no time for each other, the development of their marriage, or the care of their children. They have become victims of a disease which our friend and colleague Wayne Oates has named "workaholism." In his revealing landmark book, *Confessions of a Workaholic,* Dr. Oates defines the victim as "a person whose need for work has become so excessive that it creates noticeable disturbance or interference with his bodily health, personal happiness, and interpersonal relations, and with his smooth social functioning."[5]

While a healthy attitude toward work is indeed a foundation for our culture, *addiction to work*—the irrational pressure to achieve, to win, to acquire—pushes hard at our stress-points. And under this kind of attack, a marriage relationship can easily explode into hurtful and painful distress, or else be driven further into either a state of cold war or of studied indifference.

Denise Turner, the wife of a Baptist clergyman, paints a vivid picture of the scene: "Once upon a time, there was a minister who thought he could have it all. He believed that he could be all things to all people—if he could only work hard enough. He also believed that a fairy godmother would eventually reward him for his efforts by whisking him away to the perfect (multi-staff) church, where he could live happily ever after. It was, of course, a fairy tale.

"We started out wrong from the beginning of our marriage. We were both programmed to expect ministers to be computerized walking machines who preached, visited, counseled, studied, wrote books, attended seminars, did a little marrying on the side, and had enough spare time to lead the youth group. They were securely perched on their pedestals. Time was never a problem, we thought.

"Believing in this kind of fantasy world, we plunged into marriage with a whirlwind of activity. We juggled part-time and full-time jobs with college, graduate school, and seminary, and we acted like we knew what we were doing. Not once during those years did we slow down enough to ask why we did not know each other. It was not until we had gotten settled into our first church that we started to realize something was wrong."

Well-intentioned motives had propelled the Turners onto the workaholic treadmill with lemming-like intensity. But an awareness of the growing paralysis in their family relationship did not begin to seep through until they had a family discussion one day. Mr. Turner asked his daughter, Becky, "How about you? Do you think Daddy spends enough time with you?"

"Who's Daddy?" she answered, only partially kidding.

Her response triggered a recognition that some changes must be made if their own relationship was to be preserved and enriched, and if they as spiritual leaders in their community were to model a healthy marriage and family style. "From that day on, we began to work at solving our time management problems."[6]

Unfortunately, work obsession, even in something as worthy as church activities, is not limited to the clergy. We have known many people who have similarly neglected marriage and family in their misplaced efforts to serve the cause of their church or civic organization. Ted Engstrom and David Juroe have observed: "Church people are taught to decry idolatry in any form. They can quote the Ten Commandments on this subject. But the irony is that many of them make religious work an idolatry in itself, at the expense of other areas of life."[7]

This same work malady can carry over into other worthwhile social and civic activities as well. Marriage and family are frequently neglected by people who, for whatever reason, become so absorbed in good causes that everything else takes a back seat. Again quoting from Engstrom and Juroe: "Volunteerism can be another beautiful form of escape. It is the cloak or mantle. It may be the most severe form of the workaholic disease, because it gives the appearance of godly dedication and do-goodism."[8]

Dual-Career Work Stress

To further compound the work stress on the marriage relationship, the last half of the twentieth century has seen an unprecedented entry of women into the work force. In 1958 there were 9.3 million families in the United States where both the husband and wife worked outside the home. In 1978, just twenty years later, that figure jumped to a total of 19.4 million American families where both the husband and wife were holding down jobs. And in the twelve to fifteen years since then, while the percentage of increase has slowed down somewhat, the fact remains that in today's world, it is the rule rather than the exception for both husband and wife to be working outside the home.

It is not our purpose here to examine the many factors that lie behind this increase in dual-career marriages. However, this we know for sure: a whole new set of stresses engulfs the home where both husband and wife are working, and most of us are ill-prepared to cope with them. A classic example of one form of stress that can plague the dual-career relationship comes through in the story of Sylvia and Cecil Cooper.

Scene 6—Sylvia and Cecil

Sylvia and Cecil were both sixty-four, but they looked and acted ten years younger. Cecil was an account executive in a large advertising agency, and Sylvia worked as an administrative assistant to the vice president of a magazine publishing company. They both agreed that the major crisis in their married lives had occurred several years before, when Sylvia had been working for the director of public relations at the publishing company.

"At that time I was working for Wilbur Bradley, our director of PR. Wilbur was a master manipulator of people, and I was running hard to prove that I could do anything he asked me to do—and do it better than even he thought I could. He traveled a lot, so when he was gone, I would just take over. And when he was in town, he often called me at night, and I would run back to the office and work with him for another couple of hours. Then quite often I would go to the office on Saturdays and Sundays in order to keep up with the heavy backlog of paperwork. I was hell-bent on being Miss Efficiency. It was hard, and I knew I was neglecting my family, but at the same time all that rushing around and being needed made me feel important.

Wilbur used to say that I was the greatest, and I would do most anything to prove that he was right.

"As I look back now, I can see that I was on a treadmill. But the funny thing was that I didn't want off. One night Cecil took the phone off the hook, sat me down in a chair, and said that we were going to have a talk; and we did!"

Cecil picked up on the story. "I'd been building up to this for a long time. Sylvia wasn't getting home from the office until almost seven o'clock at night, and then she often turned up missing on the weekends. The boys and I missed her terribly, and we just didn't have any home life. I had tried to discuss this problem with her before, but she always managed to sidetrack the conversation.

"But I was desperate. I believed our marriage of twenty-five years was in deep trouble. So I demanded that she tell Wilbur, by ten o'clock the next morning, that she was through working for him. I didn't care whether she quit her job completely or took a transfer to another department. Now, that was really out of character for me because Sylvia and I have an equal partnership marriage. Normally, we don't issue ultimatums to each other."

"Boy, was I mad!" Sylvia cut in. "I didn't like the ultimatum one bit. It was the first time he had ever done that. I screamed and argued, but he wouldn't give an inch. It's funny, though, deep down underneath I think I knew he was right, but I just wasn't used to being ordered around. So I pouted and flounced off to bed without saying another word.

"I was still mad the next morning, but I had done a lot of thinking instead of sleeping. My pride was hurt, but as soon as Wilbur arrived at the office, I told him I wanted a transfer. Fortunately, there was an opening for my present job, so I made the change. Within a couple of weeks I could see the difference and was glad Cecil had forced my hand."

Cecil had the last word: "I'm still not sure I handled it right. There might have been a better way. But the important thing is that we weathered the crisis, and all I can say is, I'm one lucky guy."

By the time we left the Coopers' home that night we decided they were both lucky. But on second thought, we doubt that luck has much to do with their relationship. Here were two people who had worked hard at their marriage and had faced a work crisis of tremendous importance. Because of their deep commitment to each other, Cecil had been willing to take what for him was a desperate risk. But then, there's a lot of risk in a couple's commitment to each other, and with Cecil and Sylvia, their obvious happiness was the payoff.

Defusing the Work Bomb

The value of work—the importance of healthy achieving, of feeling needed, the satisfaction that comes from contributing to the good of society, the earning of money to provide for our families—certainly is unquestioned by most people. But it is possible that Western civilization has become guilty of a creeping work aberration that places a greater emphasis on quantity than on quality. In addition, the information revolution and the innovations in modern technology have produced drastic changes in the work scene, contributing to our stress and anxiety about keeping up.

Within this milieu, virtually everyone we talked with felt that work problems and concerns exacted a heavy stress toll on their relationship. Most everyone admitted to recurring scenes of conflict. Some were able to avoid the damaging consequences of distress most of the time; others could not. What seemed to make the difference?

Certainly, these differences are complex and involve various ingredients of a total lifestyle. And there are many different ways to approach the resolving of the differences and conflicts that are brought on by certain work attitudes and habits. But from our conversations there emerged two primary points that we believe offer a solid base for defusing the potentially dangerous work bomb threatening so many marriages and families today.

First, the married couples who seemed to have a handle on managing work stress were keenly aware that unless a proper balance was maintained between work and all other aspects of their lives, distress and conflict were likely to occur. In other words, these couples were conscious that their relationships were under daily stress, resulting from the demands of their work. This awareness then set the stage for the caring and committed couple to work toward a creative response to the stress.

Second, and of equal importance, is a couple's willingness to talk through a work-stress problem as it occurs. This, of course, involves much that we've already said about communication. But as with money stress issues, work stress plagues most of us 365 days a year. The burying of differences of opinion, hurt feelings, and hostility only asks for a violent and damaging eruption. Perhaps the hardest lesson I've had to learn is that when things get tense at our house, it is time to talk. Awareness and communication, I'm coming to realize, are the beginning points to the resolving of our differences and avoiding possible distress. Evelyn Duvall sums it up:

> One of the critical tests of the adequacy of the communication established within a marriage is found in the way in which the two people meet in a conflict situation. As long as they keep silent and pretend they have no problems, little progress can be made in getting through to each other. When one person leaves the conflict situation in anger or tears or in patient

martyrdom, communication between the partners is poor. As the husband and wife make a real effort to share their true feelings and to accept without anxiety or fear the fact that their feelings and values do differ, they are able to learn to bridge their differences."[9]

Chapter Ten

The Best Half of Life?

*Middle age is a time for discovery, not stagnation.
It is a time ripe for fresh beginnings—a threshold
to a rich and stimulating future. If approached
with good humor, flexibility, and an openness to
change, the middle years and beyond can be the
best half of life.*   Floyd and Harriett Thatcher

Living through and beyond the middle-age years is a quite
recent phenomenon with which most of us are a little ill at
ease. We are grateful for each added year, but wish somehow we could discover how to live them with a style and
meaning that would dispel the haunting feeling that life
has gone on and left us behind.

With the passing years there seems frequently to be a
kind of monotonous flatness—a dull, ordinary quality—to
so much of life. We become trapped in ruts that at first were
comfortable, but as they are cut deeper over the years, we
begin to feel smothered and walled in.

By midlife, a subtle corrosion has eaten away at the
marriage relationship, and many couples in their forties
and fifties become aware that slowly and steadily they
have grown apart. Satisfaction with marriage has declined.
They don't talk or interact as much as they did during the
earlier years, and there is little indication of common
interests.

Now and then we see a married couple who appears to
have made it through the first twenty or so years of married

life into middle age without massive emotional scars or marital collapse or settling, out of convenience, for a third- or fourth-rate relationship. But the recent findings of marriage research teams still point to widespread marital dissatisfaction with the passing years. And the startling late divorce statistics headline a frightening threat to the possibility of a creative, long-term marriage relationship.

Unique Midlife Pressures

A glaring fact of life today can be seen in an unprecedented acceleration in broken marriages among men and women in their forties and fifties. While statistics are usually cold and boring, there are flesh and blood, hurt and broken dreams packaged in the government figures that report that the divorce rate for persons forty-five and older almost doubled between 1964 and 1974—from 164,000 to 315,000 divorces granted.

It was, of course, the painful awareness of the breakdown of twenty-year-plus marriages that cut through Harriett and me to the point that made us ask apprehensively: Can this happen to us? And in response to this question we began our search for signals and signs that seem to spell out some possible answers. It soon became apparent to us that the marriage relationship is subjected to certain types of pressure and stress unique to the middle years. Most of us approach this time of life with feelings of anxiety and insecurity. The subtle physical and emotional pressures seem to carry the ingredients for a damaging kind of explosive distress which could result in impaired relationships.

While all of our interviews touched in varying degrees on the stress of midlife on the marriage relationship, two in particular were devoted almost entirely to this time. Both couples we talked with were about halfway through the middle years period of their lives.

Scene 1—Peter and Rachel

We had looked forward to meeting Peter and Rachel Hurley. Peter and Rachel lived on a little side street paralleling Ocean Avenue in Myrtle Beach, South Carolina. There was a quiet charm about their white frame home we found appealing. Its umbrella of tall pines cast a scent into the air which blended with the salty tang of the ocean breeze and produced, for us, happy memories of long vacation days spent in this delightful resort setting.

Peter at fifty-three and Rachel at fifty-one appeared to be very much at ease with their life and surroundings. But it hadn't always been that way. "Before coming here we lived in Charlotte, where it was just expected that we would stay right there," Peter explained. "I had a good job with an insurance company and was ambitious to get ahead. Before we were married and for a time after, Rachel worked as a legal secretary in one of Charlotte's oldest and most prestigious law firms. We both worked hard and made good money, but we still had time to hit the social scene—church, country club, Junior League, the whole bit. I'd go anywhere and do almost anything to meet new people—potential clients, you know."

Rachel then picked up on the story. "After a couple of years we agreed that it was time to start the family. I stopped work in my sixth month of pregnancy and concentrated all my energies on getting ready for the baby. Then after Susan was born I settled down to get our routines going the way I thought they should. I was quite a perfectionist in those days, so it was important for me to get our lives organized and scheduled.

"When Susan was born, Peter and I decided that we'd wait about a year and then plan for a second child. Everything worked according to our time schedule, and our son, Rex, was born when Susan was a little over two years old. It was all neat and tidy. Now we had our family and could settle down to being successful in our social and business worlds."

Alternating back and forth for almost three hours, Rachel and Peter unraveled their story. Peter had struggled up the insurance company ladder, and by the time he was thirty-five he had become a member of the Million Dollar Round Table. His workdays averaged between twelve and fifteen hours. On Saturdays it was golf or tennis with colleagues and potential clients. Most of the time they made church on Sunday mornings; that was part of being respected and accepted in Charlotte. And Sunday afternoons were invariably devoted to social engagements of one kind or another. They were seldom alone.

With her customary drive Rachel moved through her days as super-mother, plus the bridge club, Junior League, hospital volunteering, P.T.A., and fund-raising for the Civic Art Committee. And while all of this was going on, she played the first-class wife game. Office responsibilities demanded entertaining Peter's colleagues and clients—that's how you got ahead. And they both dabbled in church activities just enough to keep that relationship alive.

During their growing-up years Susan and Rex sort of made it on their own. In a conversation later with Susan she said, "Rex and I were normal kids, I guess. We didn't see much of Mom and Dad and there wasn't a lot of family togetherness, but we knew we were loved. I think we both felt, though, that there was something missing. Some of our friends seemed to have a close family life—the kind we thought we would enjoy."

Rachel recalled Peter's fortieth birthday: "I wondered what all of the fuss was about when Peter turned forty. He was in a blue funk for weeks. I thought it was kind of funny when he moaned and groaned about being middle-aged. After all, one birthday doesn't all of a sudden make a person middle-aged. But then a couple of years later I hit the same kind of low, and it wasn't a bit funny. I began to feel anxious and concerned about myself and my world. It seemed like no matter how hard I tried I couldn't get rid of my feelings of insecurity, and it wasn't something I felt Peter and I could discuss.

"I worried about whether Peter still found me attractive as a woman. Even though I tried to watch my weight, I didn't like what I saw in the mirror. It really got to be a thing with me. I knew that our sex life wasn't always satisfactory to Peter. Over the years I had never given satisfactory sex the same importance he had. And there were times when I'd wake up in the middle of the night with a tight feeling in my stomach after dreaming that Peter had left me for one of the younger women in his office. This went on for almost five years, and I was miserable.

"The children didn't need me like they once did. Peter was working harder and longer than ever, and I felt lost and alone. While I kept busy with volunteer work and club activities, I still had this empty, hollow feeling. We were all going our separate ways and nobody seemed to need me anymore."

Peter had been listening quietly to Rachel's side of the story, but now he broke in, "Let me tell you what was going on with me during those years. At times the pressures at the office were almost more than I could handle. Even though I had always felt very self-confident and success had come early, I started to question my own abilities. Younger men were coming up fast in the company, and I began to wonder if I could keep up with them. A couple of my associates were passed up for promotion by younger men, and I worried about whether that would happen to me. So I worked harder and longer, but it wasn't fun anymore. The old drive was gone, and it didn't take much for me to feel tired.

"I was afraid of my feelings—afraid of what seemed to be happening to me. And I began to feel very insecure about our marriage relationship. We'd had a good thing once, but now I wondered.

"One Friday afternoon I left the office around two o'clock and drove over to a little park. It was quiet and peaceful, and I sat on the bench for a couple of hours just thinking. For the first time in years I was aware of the sound of the breeze as it rustled through the trees. I was aware of the birds singing, and in the distance I could hear the laughter of children. Through it all I thought about Rachel and our life together. It seemed like we had lost touch with the real world around us. Our relationship had really gotten sour. I wasn't the least bit happy, and I wondered how she felt.

"After wrestling for a couple of hours with the questions that had tormented my mind for months, an idea hit me, and I rushed back to the car and headed for home. Rachel and I had to talk. We hadn't really talked to each other for years, but somehow I knew we had to now. My excitement held until I pulled into the driveway, and then I wondered how she would feel. Would she think I was crazy? I didn't know, but I had to find out."

It was Rachel's turn. "Boy, was I surprised when Peter arrived home at 4:30 in the afternoon. My first thought was that something was terribly wrong at the office or he was sick, but the look on his face said something different. And when he suggested that just the two of us drive to Spartanburg for the weekend, I couldn't believe what I was hearing. We hadn't done much of anything together for years, but I sensed his feelings of urgency, and within an hour or so we had packed up and were on the road.

"We talked all the way to Spartanburg, and then after we got settled in our hotel we talked far into the night until we were both exhausted. And on Saturday morning we started again. The hesitancy we had felt at first soon melted away as we expressed our anxieties and insecurities and our feeling that life was passing us by and that we had forgotten how to live. We talked and laughed and cried and made love. And then on Sunday we dreamed and made plans."

"But to get back to what for me was a scary part of the story," Peter cut in, "I talked with my boss on Monday morning and asked for a transfer to the company's Myrtle Beach office. I shared the struggle we'd been going through, and while I don't think he could really identify with us, he was at least sympathetic. Within a couple of months everything was worked out. We sold our home in Charlotte and bought this place. Professionally, it was a comedown for me, and I had to take a slight cut in salary at first, but it has been worth it.

"The transition has been hard at times. It took us a couple of years to adjust to our new lifestyle, and we had to get acquainted with each other all over again. I don't think either of us realized just how far apart we had drifted. We had each gone our own way and done our own thing for years. But now we are learning to share our life together in a new way. The masks are off most of the time, and we're closer and more in love than I think we've ever been.

"And as for my work, the pace is slower here. I don't have any feeling of being on a treadmill or of having to be involved in petty office politics, and the pressures are much less than they were in Charlotte.

"Another thing we have noticed is a deepening in the quality of our relationships with other people. While we still do some business entertaining, most of our social times are spent with close friends we enjoy being with. We're together because we want to be, not because of some business or social angle. Our circle of friends is much broader since we've become active in the church again, and I know that our spiritual values have deepened."

Our hours with Peter and Rachel convinced us that the decisions they made on that Spartanburg weekend were right for them. They had weathered a painful midlife transition and had come up with answers that opened up a new and exciting life.

This doesn't mean, of course, that other couples could or should try to mimic their pattern for coping and for change. For most people it might not be practical. But we have come to feel that what happened in the *reevaluating* and *revitalizing* of their relationship can be crucial to an ongoing marriage that makes it into and through the emotionally difficult middle years.

Scene 2—Hal and Florence

Hal and Florence Perkins were fifty-one and forty-nine when we met them. Hal was a prominent cardiologist on staff at one of the major hospitals in the vast medical complex located on Houston's south side. He was tall and distinguished looking in a well-tailored brown suit with plaid design. But the vertical worry or frown line above his nose was etched deep, and there was a tenseness about him which put us on guard at first.

Florence looked perfect for her role as a wife of a successful doctor—tall, feminine, engaging smile, the epitome of charm. Yet we could see that she was restless and uneasy.

During the years that Hal was struggling with his studies in medical school, Florence taught history in one of the local high schools. She had apparently been a capable and well-liked teacher, and it was her income that paid the bills during Hal's medical school years.

"I continued working for a year after Hal went on staff at the hospital, and then I quit because I was pregnant. While those school years were difficult and we didn't have much money, Hal and I were happy. Our dreams for the future kept us going.

"Hal and I had been raised in the same small town. We both came from devout Baptist homes and carried those roots and spiritual values into our early life together. We were very much in love and felt especially close when our daughter, Wendy, was born. And even though Hal was beginning to get extremely busy at the hospital, we still found time to do things together.

"I remember those as the happiest days of my life. And since Hal was beginning to do better financially, I was glad to stay home and be wife and mother. But after a year or two things began to change. Hal's hours got longer and more demanding. He even spent most of every weekend at the hospital. And then when Wendy started school, I was suddenly faced with time on my hands. So in desperation I went back to teaching and divided myself between that and being a mother to Wendy for the next seven or eight years.

"But then I realized I was getting bored and short-tempered. The kids at school began to get on my nerves, so I quit and decided to try staying home. By this time Wendy was a teenager, and I felt I should be around when she was home. It wasn't long, though, before I was climbing the walls. I had to do something so I began to play bridge two or three days a week with a group of doctor's wives. Most of them were just like I was—bored and dissatisfied. We were all lonely and unhappy because of the long hours our husbands put in at the hospital.

"When Hal and I were together, which wasn't often, it seemed that we spent more time arguing than anything else. We disagreed about almost everything—how we spent our money, how to handle Wendy's teenage problems, his working all the time. Nothing about our life together was right, including sex. It seemed like we were in some sort of vacuum, and there's no way sex and intimacy can make it in a situation like that. But I needed desperately to feel loved, to be made to feel attractive and desirable as a woman. Some of my friends were having affairs, and there was one time when I came awfully close because I was so lonely, but I just couldn't bring myself to it."

Harriett and I had watched Florence closely during the several minutes it took for her to cover this much of the story. Strain was beginning to show in her voice and manner. Remembering the past was obviously painful, but she had seemed determined to stay with it. I felt it was time to shift the scene, so I cut in and asked Hal, "How do you feel about the last five to ten years of your marriage?"

"Before answering that I have to go back a ways. We were married young, during my first year of medical school. And I was almost thirty by the time I had finished school and served my time as an intern and resident. Those were difficult but happy years for us. She has sacrificed a lot to help me get through, and so when I got my first staff job, I was anxious to start making that up to her. I worked hard and enjoyed it. My colleagues respected me, and my patients thought I was special. So when Florence began to nag at me, I felt she was being unreasonable, that she didn't appreciate what I was trying to do for her.

"About the only time I felt happy and secure was when I was at the hospital, and except for Wendy I didn't feel appreciated at home, so I just stayed away more. Now and then I'd feel guilty and try to spend more time at home. We had some happy hours together now and then, but I'd soon get itchy and fall back into my old routine.

"Then along came my forty-fifth birthday. My fortieth birthday didn't bother me, but being forty-five was a jolt to my ego. I began to feel very insecure and unsure of myself. I had always thought I was a good doctor, but maybe I was wrong. Or if I was right, probably I'd never get any better. I felt middle-aged and over the hill, and my married life was all messed up.

"One night Florence and I got into a real shouting fight over something Wendy wanted to do. It really wasn't all that important, I guess, but all of our anger and frustration boiled to the surface. The next thing I knew Florence jumped up and said she'd had it. She didn't want to live this way anymore. Either I had to get out or she would; we were through.

"I don't know how to explain it, but even with all my feelings of hostility somehow I knew that if either of us went out that door, something really important would be lost, and I wasn't ready for that. When I asked Florence if she meant what she had said, she just started to cry. The next thing I knew I was crying too, and I hadn't done that since I was a little boy.

"That was three years ago. We've been going to a marriage counselor off and on ever since. It's still rocky, but we can talk about it now. I've cut down on my practice, and we're trying to do more things together. But it isn't easy because we had grown so far apart. We don't seem to have any common interests or dreams about the future anymore. I sometimes wonder if we'll make it, but our counselor seems to think there's some hope so we keep working at it."

Hal glanced across the room at Florence with a questioning look. Her eyes glistened a little as she said almost as if to herself, "We'll keep working at it. I think we've made some headway, but we've got a long way to go."

Then she looked over at us and said, "It has been hard to relive all this again, but Hal and I agreed that if our story would help someone else, it would be worth it. That's why we decided to talk with you."

Warning Signals

The short space given these vignettes does not reveal everything that contributed to the distress which so seriously crippled their relationships. But there appear to be some rather significant signals which may give us clues that can lead to a steady movement toward maturity and happiness with the passing years.

While Hal and Florence moved into the child-rearing and "get-ahead-years" at a later age than Peter and Rachel, *they both succumbed to the stifling and selfish pattern of burying themselves in their own little worlds.* Hal wanted to make it big, he said, as a payoff for Florence because of her work and effort during his years of training. But in the process he shut her out of his life.

Neither couple made any significant effort during their late twenties and thirties consciously to develop a pattern for doing certain things together on a regular basis. There was no apparent cultivation of mutual interests, and both admitted that they hadn't really talked to each other except in a superficial and surface manner. Feelings were buried.

We also discovered that *neither couple had given any serious thought in their earlier years to what they would face in midlife.* When I asked Rachel and Florence if they had given any thought to the time when the children would be gone and they would experience menopausal change, neither had. They just thought it would happen and they'd cope with it when it did.

And a similar response came from Peter and Hal when asked if they had given any thought to what their feelings and reactions would be as they moved into middle age. Peter said that the little he had read about the so-called "midlife crisis" made him feel that it was just a lot of foolishness. Because of his training and reading, Hal said he had thought about it some but felt it was all a psychological thing he could handle when the time came. But neither *had* handled it when it came, and their marriages suffered the agonies of crippling distress.

And so as Harriett and I reflected on these two stories and those of the many other people we talked with, and as we thought about our own marriage during the beginnings of the midlife stage, the inevitable questions surfaced:

- How can couples avoid a decline in marital satisfaction with the passing years?
- How can we handle those feelings that come at some point during the middle-age period when an awareness seeps into our thinking that at least half of our lives, if not more, is behind?
- What sort of adjustments are called for when the children are gone and a couple is alone again?
- How are we to cope with the physical and emotional changes that seem to confront married couples during their middle years?

While numerous and varied elements seem to contribute to tired and dull marriages, our findings and experiences indicate *that the gradual erosion of mutual hopes and dreams over the first twenty to twenty-five years is a subtle but deadly sign.* Nearly always there is an accompanying decline of common interests—of things to talk about and share in together. Even though a couple may hang together without change for many years, emotional divorce has occurred and deprived them of the fulfillment that is deserved in a long-term marriage relationship.

Emotional Upheaval

The emotional stresses that so frequently afflict a married couple in midlife may be brought on in large degree by the frustration and pain of coping with present change and anxiety over the inevitable changes out ahead. The Hurleys and the Perkinses talked about the difficulties each experienced emotionally and physically as they moved into middle age, but neither could trace the emotional upheaval to any single time or event. In fact, for most of us, the creeping symptoms may not even be recognized until they have become firmly entrenched in our emotional patterns. These feelings, expressed by both couples, include: a haunting anxiety that time has passed us by; fears of not quite measuring up to our early expectations; fretful anticipation of coming reverses or catastrophe; uneasy feelings of entrapment and being boxed in; an inability to make decisions; depression and insecurity; fears of illness, old age, and death.

By the same token we talked with some people who had eased into their forties, fifties, and even sixties having given little thought, so they said, to the passing years. Forty-eight-year-old Liz said, "I have to remind myself that I'm as old as I am. I don't feel it, and I know I don't look it." At fifty-one Dave said, "It never scared me. I felt like it was all in your head. You can feel as young as you want to make yourself feel and as old as you think you are." And John remembered, "It never bothered me. I can do just as many things today at sixty-five as I did at forty—maybe not for as long or as fast, but I don't have any problems with that." Mary Louise insisted, "I'm fifty, and I don't feel like I've reached middle age yet."

But in varying degrees most of us do experience at least some emotional upheaval in midlife brought on in large measure by the changes taking place in our marriage, our family, and our social lives—not to discount the physical changes we all experience.

The Children Are Gone

There is certainly no question that one of the most difficult transitions confronting a married couple in midlife occurs when the last child leaves home. And according to the American average, this is likely to happen to a couple between ages forty-five and fifty. Up to this point there is a possibility that the wife and mother has immersed herself in the routines of the home and the needs of her children, and often in a career as well. A husband and father in most cases has found deep personal satisfaction in providing most, if not all, of the financial needs and in performing certain tasks that have given him a sense of accomplishment and of being needed.

I recall so well one night years ago when our adult daughter told me about a problem that had developed with her car that day. My immediate response was, "Okay, honey, I'll be glad to take care of it for you." But then she said, "Daddy, Paul has already had it fixed." For a few moments I was crushed. I had always looked out for my daughter and her cars. Harriett wisely took me to one side and pointed out that it was only natural that Paul, Sherrill's boyfriend at the time and later her husband, would want to take care of it for her. Besides, he knew more about cars than I did. She was right, but it just took a little getting used to.

We talked with many women who admitted that when their last child left home everything seemed to fall apart. They had so funneled all their energies and time into the lives of their children that outside interests and relationships were almost nonexistent, and it seemed they were living in sort of a vacuum. The idea of an empty nest—the unknown—brought on feelings of anxiety and questions about how it would affect their relationships with their husbands.

And in many instances the relationship with their husbands had deteriorated and become less satisfying during the years preoccupied with child-rearing; on a deep emotional level husband and wife were strangers.

Scene 3—Jane

Jane Heyworth remembers: "A week or so after our last son left for college and I had finished all of the little chores related to his leaving, I realized one morning that I really had nothing to do and nowhere to go. It was a strange feeling, and I felt depressed and lonely. Bill was at a critical point in his career. He was working long hours and always dead tired when we were together. So I had to battle out my feelings alone. It took me almost a year of misery to sort things out, work through them, and find a new way of life that had meaning and satisfaction for me.

"I see now where I made one of the biggest mistakes of my life. When our kids were born, I made up my mind that I would be a super-mother. All during the years of their growing up I felt I was too busy for any outside activities. I didn't have any hobbies; I didn't even read. And Bill and I never did things together—everything was for the kids. So when they left, my world broke down.

"Like a lot of women I guess I've got 20-20 hindsight. If I had it to do over again, I'd still want to be a good mother, but I see now that doesn't mean not having a life of my own either. I was probably more of a "smother" than a mother. Even during those busy child-rearing years I think every woman should get involved in activities and interests that can carry over into the years when the children are gone. And Bill and I have often talked about the fact that we think we would have been better parents if just the two of us had done things together more. We had grown apart, but thank heavens we found our way back."

Many years ago Eleanor Roosevelt, at fifty-seven, expressed a life-fulfilling idea when she wrote:

> Somewhere along the line of development we discover what we really are and then we make our real decision for which we are responsible. Make that decision primarily for yourself, because you never really live anyone else's life, not even your own child's. The influence you exert is through your own life.[1]

It is the wise and aware parent who plans for those days of letting go. *A vital part of the parental task is to prepare children for leaving home, but of equal importance is our own preparation for that day.* And the far-seeing husband and wife will begin early to substitute new activities in their own lives to fill that inevitable gap.

The Stress of Physical and Emotional Change

To compound the stress of the empty nest, it is often at this time of life, depending on how young a couple married and the size of the family, that a woman moves into the menopause period of her life. This is a time of physical change which, while it offers the promise of freedom from pregnancy, still creates its share of frightening feelings and reactions.

The physical implications of menopause are minimized to a degree by the availability of medication which contributes toward maintaining hormonal balance. But an aware couple is sensitive to the emotional impact of this change. Any change, good or bad, produces stress, and the menopause time seems to contain both good and bad stress. *Good* because fear of pregnancy will soon be a thing of the past; demands of children are lessened; there will be more time to pursue personal interests. *Bad* because of the overwhelming concerns that produce anxiety in varying doses throughout all of the midlife years: attracting her husband sexually in spite of physical changes which she believes will make her less appealing; missing verbal affirmation from a husband who is slavishly buried in his work and who most of the time is preoccupied with his own problems at this stage; no longer feeling needed as a person by either her children or her husband; wondering what will happen to her sex life following menopause (it hasn't been too satisfying during the child-rearing years; what happens now?).

At the same time her husband is struggling with the confusing questions which now threaten his feelings of accomplishment and security. The secure and safe world which was his at thirty-five and forty has now changed, and he finds himself waking up in the middle of the night with unexplainable knots in his stomach. He is shaken by the feeling that it is possible he has peaked professionally; there are younger men who may threaten his position of authority and his world; his memory isn't as sharp as it once was, and at times he even has trouble remembering the names of his friends; climbing stairs, walking, or jogging uphill produces shortness of breath; occasional experiences of impotency strike fear at the thought of future performance in bed. All of these feelings cast a pall over the future.

This mixed bag of complex feelings is crammed with negative reactions which chip away at a man's sense of self-esteem. At a time in life when he feels he should be able to relax and enjoy the results of his years of work and an eased financial burden, feelings that he's slipping—physically, sexually, and intellectually—can create deep distress and what writers have labeled the "midlife crisis."

Henry Still points out:

> This complex time in a man's life originates from two
> major aspects of life: a decline in *sexual potency* and
> *physical strength* and abnormal concern with *profes-*
> *sional accomplishment*. The two are closely related and
> interlocked. They often coincide with the time when
> children leave home or with the loss of a loved one.
> Psychologists recognize the midlife crisis as a time of
> profound depression, especially for men who have
> set high goals for themselves. The way each man
> copes with this depression and other coincident
> symptoms determines in large measure how he will
> live out the rest of his life.[2]

Our findings point to an obvious fact that not every man
and woman experiences all of the feelings described here,
but virtually everyone we talked with admitted to feeling
some of them in varying degrees. And when it comes to
men, reactions ranged from instances like my compulsive
need at forty-eight for a red convertible, to leaving wife
and family in an effort to recapture youth and sexual
fulfillment with another partner.

Preparation for the Midlife Transition

Now we come to the key question: How does a couple
prepare for and work through the profound changes that
surface at midlife? In a sense, that is what this whole book
is about. Of primary importance, it seems to us, *is a sensitive and caring awareness of the feelings each partner will
experience or is struggling with now.*

A caring husband with a sense of purpose to remain
married becomes aware and sensitive to the physical and
emotional struggles his wife is feeling at midlife—feelings

of unexplainable anxiety, of irritation without apparent cause, of guilt or remorse over lost opportunities—and responds with love and understanding and reassurance.

At the same time a caring wife is aware, through whatever means, of the feelings of insecurity in her husband—frustrations over physical change, fear about being over the hill and having failed to meet earlier expectations, imagined loss of mental astuteness, and myriad other real or imagined shortcomings—and provides the support and reassurance that can help her husband through this time of change.

A Time to Redesign Life

But with all of the unique pressures couples face in early midlife, it is still an ideal time to redesign life. Work pressures differ from those at an earlier age. Money stress has usually diminished to some degree. Demands on the marriage by children in the home have either ceased or will shortly. Material needs have changed. In a very real sense the middle-aged person stands on the threshold of an entirely new life. What has worked in the past doesn't necessarily apply now. Psychologist Carl G. Jung underlined this truth in poetic language years ago when he wrote:

> Thoroughly unprepared we take the step into the afternoon of life; worse still, we take this step with the false supposition that our truths and ideals will serve us hitherto. But we cannot live in the afternoon of life according to the program of life's morning—for what was great in the morning will be little at evening, and what in the morning was true will at evening have become a lie.[3]

The good news here, and it was true in our experience, is that if a couple has permitted their marriage to drift into a stale, dull routine during their thirties and forties, *positive steps toward redesign and renewal at midlife can reverse the process—provided both husband and wife want it to happen.* Usually, this redesign and renewal is demanding, perhaps painful, but always rewarding. It calls for individual openness to change, a willingness to do new things and to throw off the old habits and ways of doing things that have accumulated over the years. And while this is stressful, it is the first step to recapturing the excitement that was experienced during the honeymoon period. Reuel Howe has written, "The answer to middle-aged doldrums, however, is not to go back, but to *move forward,* and, in so doing, to find in each moment its deeper meaning and possibilities."[4]

Adapting to the Second Half of Life

To capture the spirit of this renewal and revitalization step is a part of a couple's steady march toward maturity. Midlife is a time for modifying beliefs and attitudes, of redefining and enlarging ideas, and of stretching capabilities. And in so doing life's patterns are adapted to a changing environment. "This adaptability is not only desirable for advancement, but is necessary for survival."[5]

We like the way writer Nancy Mayer expressed it when she wrote:

> Despite the fact that it is much more difficult to renegotiate an old marital contract than to make a new one with someone else, this is the challenge facing midlife couples who want to revitalize their relationship: To the extent that either of them has grown and changed, they will have to hammer out

a new contract that accommodates these changes—
a new bargain, based on old routes, but purged of
old rules.[6]

Harriett and I recall so well the complex and confusing
emotions that flooded us when I was forty-five and she
was forty-two. At that time we found ourselves in new
surroundings, and our child-rearing days were over. If the
statistics applied to us, we had already lived half of our
married life and possibly between one-half and two-thirds
of our lives. For a time this was a depressing idea.

But we began to see that if we had lived half of our
married life to that point, it simply meant that *we also had
the whole second half out ahead*. What a great idea! And so,
as we've already written, we set out to develop new and
enlarged patterns for our life together. And in so many
ways, the last fifteen years have been the greatest we've
had. We've experienced the excitement of doing new things
together—of sticking our necks out—and of having fun.

Kate White asked Walter and Betty Cronkite if there had
been any real secret to keeping their marriage going strong
for forty years. "There's no secret," Betsy remarked. "I
think one thing that has helped is our senses of humor, the
fact that we've always had fun together. Even in our earlier
days in New York, when we had no money, we would take
the subway to the beach at dawn."[7]

Harriett and I have discovered that it is never too late to
"take the subway to the beach at dawn" and embrace life
together.

Plan for Growth

No two people are going to set out to live their lives
together in a way that will lead them deliberately toward times of intense crisis or marital collapse. But

unfortunately for so many couples, at the time of the wedding and the first fifteen years or so after, there is usually little thought, if any, given to planning for the maintenance of their own relationship and for their individual growth as persons.

Jane and Bill Heyworth buried themselves in the immediate tasks of child-rearing and making good in the business world, which are noble aspirations. Peter and Rachel Hurley and Hal and Florence Perkins, with the best of intentions, followed a similar pattern in their marriage and family life. But in each case, *the neglect of personal growth through widened and expanded interests and activities, and the failure to deliberately budget for time and fun together away from the rest of the family, left them as strangers in a marital vacuum.* None of these couples was prepared for the climactic morning when it was just the two of them at the breakfast table and neither knew what to say.

Robert Havighurst emphasizes the importance of conscious planning by a couple during the earlier years of their marriage when he writes, "People can be happy and free and young in spirit in their middle age and for a long time afterward if they do some personal stocktaking and planning for this period in their lives."[8]

Sex at Midlife

This same thoughtful and caring attitude certainly applies to the sexual stress that also confronts a couple during these years. We have often pondered the seeming incongruity that a man peaks sexually in his late teens and twenties while a woman's sense of gratification moves toward a peak in the late thirties, the forties, or even the fifties. It seems like sort of an unfair arrangement, doesn't it? But if we're wise, we'll let that dilemma rest with the Creator who planned it all and move on toward a complete husband-wife relationship, which God set in motion and pronounced "very good." And we believe that phrase is descriptive of sexual happiness in midlife—and beyond.

Unfortunately, midlife couples tend to settle down and relax with what is familiar. This pattern frequently deteriorates into boredom. Going through the motions is never satisfying on a deep, emotional level and in time can produce intensely distressful reactions. In contrast, however, is what some psychologists refer to as "performance anxiety." As psychologist Judd Marmor has observed:

> Men and women in our culture, regardless of their "creative love" for one another, are often caught up in fears that they will not be able to perform well sexually and that they will be unable to satisfy their partner. As a consequence of this anxiety, they become self-conscious about how they are functioning—they become "spectators" of their own sexual reactions. This combination of performance anxiety and self-consciousness acts to dilute or abort the eroticism of the encounter and results in impaired sexual function.[9]

Sex at any age in life is to be enjoyed with abandon as a deep expression of married love. To reduce this to a concern with performance is a sin against two people who are deeply committed in love to each other. As Rex Barlow said in one of our interviews, "Sex is a giving and sharing act for both of us. I think we both try to be sensitive to each other's needs as well as our own." There's no hint of a performance syndrome here.

One of the fallacies about couples approaching midlife and beyond is that sexual fervor declines. We found no evidence of this in the people we talked with— and the oldest couple were in their mid-seventies. Rather, the circumstances that can impair satisfaction for a woman and produce impotency in men are essentially the same for a couple no matter what stage of life they are in: disharmony in the marriage, work stress, lack of communication, preoccupation with one's own selfish wants and needs, just to mention some of the most obvious.

A Time of Mental Agility and Emotional Flexibility

Another bit of good news for the couple approaching middle age or already deeply entrenched in it, is the explosion of the fallacy that a person at this time of life is over the hill mentally. If mental capacity deteriorates under normal circumstances, the condition may very well have been self-induced, brought on by destructive attitudes. Developmentalist Bernice Neugarten suggests that "aging, per se, at least between forty and sixty-five, does not result in decreasing mental or emotional flexibility."[10]

Some of the "youngest" friends we have are in their fifties and sixties, and some of the oldest acting people we know are in their thirties and forties. Age is not a determining factor; *it is attitudes and relationships and flexibility.*

Frequently it is during these years as persons and as married couples that a "my way is the best way" attitude emerges. Our attitudes become concretized and fixed; we baptize our prejudices and call them convictions. And all of this becomes poison to the marriage relationship, as an awareness of life's grays is lost and a "black and white" attitude rises to the top. I once heard Dr. Paul Tournier say, "It is a sign of adolescence when you see things in black and white." Adolescent marriage at midlife is a disaster. Attitudes and relationships hinge on flexibility—a trait that so often begins to fade during the middle years because of a growing inventory of experience.

The Challenge of the Middle Years

As we reflected on our interviews, on people we've known over the years, and on our own personal experience, we have isolated for our satisfaction certain qualities that seem to make it possible to sustain a long-term marriage through and beyond the middle years. These are:

1. *An avid pursuit of individual and mutual interests.* We all need to be involved in doing certain things that are expressive of our personality and that offer an opportunity to expand our creativity—something that is specifically our own. For some it may be painting or writing or gourmet cooking. For others it may be knitting or sewing or photography or making furniture. And as married couples, we need to discover activities that draw us together in common interests and give expression to our combined enjoyment and creative abilities—learning a new foreign language, playing bridge or backgammon, fishing, playing golf, team-teaching in church, sailing, rock hunting.

2. *The discovery of a desire for a new and expanded togetherness.* Some call it intimacy. But whatever we call it, the masks come off in favor of sharing and expressing love on a deep level. And this finds expression in such little things as a Saturday night date once or twice a month, or meeting for lunch together at noon once a week, or a planned weekend together at some favorite spot once every two or three months. Togetherness physically, emotionally, and mentally is spelled out with a sharing of deep feelings, a mutual exploring of needs and hopes, and in the doing of things that stretch our capabilities as a couple.

3. *The expansion and deepening of our relationships with friends.* The cultivation of a wide range and variety of friendships

makes us more interesting people. And this can contribute to a couple being more interesting to each other. It is through meaningful friendships that a couple receives the warmth of being loved and needed, and their lives are enriched through shared experiences and feelings of support. The person at midlife has a vast and rich reservoir of experiences and relationships to draw from which can give spice and meaning and quality to friendships.

4. *A lively sense of humor.* We desperately need the ability to see humor in the daily routines of life and not to take ourselves too seriously. The dullest people we've known are those who seem to be painfully serious about all of life around them—themselves included. It's rather strange, though, that while a few people appear to have things figured out so they're able to see the funny side of life, for most of us it is an acquired art—something we have to work at, a set of the mind.

5. *A more creative understanding of time.* Ingrained in each of us during the middle years is the yearning to reflect and reevaluate. But the hurly-burly pace of today's world so clutters our minds that we find it difficult, if not impossible, to concentrate on anything but superficial details. Eric Hoffer has a penetrating way to get to the heart of things when he writes, "The superficiality of the American is the result of his hustling. It needs leisure to think things out; it needs leisure to mature. People in a hurry cannot think, cannot grow, nor can they decay. They are preserved in a state of perpetual puerility."[11] These years are a time for reflection and for taking a second look at our values.

6. *A sensitivity to moral and spiritual values.* Many we talked with found a deep sense of meaning as a couple in their

moral values and in their religious faith. Some credited their faith with helping to hold their marriages together in difficult times. And there were those whose marriages had been fractured even though they had lived and practiced their faith over the years. But the findings of others and ourselves attest to the binding qualities of faith and a daily expression of religious beliefs:

> Research studies show that in general, in our culture, the presence of a religious faith is associated with more favorable chances for marital success.... Studies covering approximately 25,000 marriages have shown that there were three times as many marital failures among people with no religious affiliation as among those within given religions.[12]

Over 80 percent of the people we interviewed believed that their faith and attendance at church or synagogue was an important ingredient to the success of their marriages. While Harriett and I do not credit our religious faith and beliefs as the sole reason for the success of our marriage for over fifty years, we both find that it is vitally important to us as persons and as a couple.

Prime Time

But there's a happy contrast to the gloomy statistics on marriage breakup at midlife. Increasing numbers of couples are learning to handle the stresses of their marital relationship and turn that last half of life into Prime Time. They are effectively making them into the "best years of their lives" through planning, commitment, and a realistic, practical, and sometimes whimsical view of middle age. We like what our friend Robert Raines says:[13]

Middle-agers are beautiful!
  aren't we, Lord?
I feel for us
  too radical for our parents
  too reactionary for our kids
Supposedly in the prime of life
  like prime rib
  everybody eating off me
    devouring me
  nobody thanking me
    appreciating me
but still hanging in there
  communicating with my parents
  in touch with my kids
and getting more in touch
  with myself
and that's all good
  Thanks for making it good
and
  could you make it a little better?

Chapter 11

Marriage and Retirement

*The retirement years are hand-holding times, a
time for hugs, a time for saying "I love you," a
time for affirming each other.*

Floyd and Harriett Thatcher

"I married him for better or worse, but not for lunch!"
muttered a harried and frustrated wife. Her words and the
rasp in her voice were a glaring testimony to her struggle
with the prosaic and exasperating routine of having her
newly retired husband underfoot all day—including breakfast, lunch, and dinner.

When we first heard that acerbic comment, it made little
impression on us. At the time we were in our midlife
marriage years, and still caught up in the work-a-day
grind that put spice into our way of life. As a matter of fact,
we wrote the prior chapter on the "Best Half of Life" and
completed the first edition of this book during those midlife years.

But now, fifteen years later, it's a different story. I have
shed the daily office routine and corporate life, and Harriett and I have moved into the role of a "retired" married
couple—a time sometimes referred to as "the third age."
How does a couple go about preparing for and enjoying
the huge changes that come with this third age?

Throughout this book we have exposed our personal feelings and reactions as we have discussed our ongoing search for those ingredients that go into making a satisfying and rewarding lifetime marriage. And while we've shared at length the experiences of others, we can best answer that question by focusing now exclusively on our own retirement journey and how it has affected our marriage relationship.

Change—Who Wants It!

Upon plunging into the retirement world, some of the people we know set up a shop or office away from home. But without thinking too much about it we decided to convert a spare bedroom into my office. Outfitted with bookshelves and the necessary furniture, my workplace was located just four feet from our bedroom and about twenty-five feet from our much lived-in family room—all within earshot. Harriett now had me for better, for worse, *and* for lunch.

Were we prepared for this major change in our lives?

As a lifetime married couple, the flip answer to that question is "yes." The thoughtful and honest answer is "not really." Yes, in the sense that we had prepared ourselves financially as best we could. But in retrospect, we were not prepared emotionally. There was a deep abyss between our heads and our hearts. In reality we were reluctant to accept the fact that we were growing older and were actually on the brink of that big step into the retirement world.

One observer of this reluctance has observed, "There are four stages in life: childhood, youth, middle age, and the 'you're looking good' stage."[1] When we are greeted by old friends we haven't seen for several years and they give us that "My, you're looking good" routine, we are forced to admit that, indeed, we must be moving into this fourth stage of life.

No Guidelines

Michael Montaigne, the French essayist, observed, "To retire successfully is no easy matter." He was so right. As a professional workaholic for over forty-five years, I felt a choking sense of panic, along with a certain amount of anticipation, as we set a specific date for my change of status. Like most men and women in today's world, my identity had been wrapped up in my active professional life. Without meaning to, I had become victimized by the notion that "what I do is who I am."

The big question surged to the surface of my thinking: Could I handle the change? Harriett assured me in no uncertain terms that I could. But in spite of her confidence, I would frequently awaken in the black hours of the night with a burning stomach and a cold sweat.

We have long been followers of Norman Peale's "positive thinking." That, along with my Christian faith, moved me toward the reality that the unknown ahead had to be explored, even though the "guidelines for retiring" were a bit fuzzy.

Retirement, as we know it, is a comparatively new phenomenon. Until the last three or four generations, life expectancy was shorter and most folks worked until they died or were otherwise incapacitated. The average age expectancy in the 1940s was 65.9 years. Now we can look forward to at least an additional sixteen years, and the United States Bureau of Statistics indicates this is increasing steadily. As we write this, about one in eight Americans is over sixty-five. These facts reveal that more of us will be facing the challenges of keeping our marriages vibrant as we grow old together.

A New Pattern Emerges

Back to our journey. Our exploration of this third age drove us to read everything we could find that would expand our understanding and our horizons. I have long been an avid reader of the Royal Bank of Canada Monthly Letter, which offers timely advice. I carefully stash away most of them for future reference. One article was especially apt: "Retirement is to be looked upon as the beginning of a new life experience. But no formula will fit everyone." In other words, there are no pat answers. *Each person and each couple must develop a pattern that is satisfying to them.*

Another insightful gem was particularly helpful: "Retirement does not require us to abandon interests and activities wholesale, but merely to change the emphasis and reassess the values we assign to various enterprises in our daily lives. Think of retirement positively. It is not loafing or withdrawing, but participating in life a new way."[2] The popular and astute television personality Hugh Downs picked up on this same idea: "The sensible person doesn't really retire. He or she changes activities or occupations. One who retires to do something else, to live life in a positive, new way, is still in command."[3]

I may have done too much in my effort to stay in command, as Harriett observed: "I could tell Floyd took all of this advice to heart, because during the last few months of his official office life, he furiously planned and plotted the first twelve months of his retirement with a breathless schedule of consultation and speaking and teaching engagements. It was obvious to me that he was overdoing it. But, let's face it, we hadn't been over this road before, so I couldn't be sure just what it would take to make the adjustment."

I did go overboard, but the transition worked out for us beautifully. Six months into that first year of retirement brought in an editorial and writing assignment that filled my time for the next eight years. My "retirement" became a time of doing what I knew best.

Harriett came up with a saying that was so right: "You have to *learn* to grow older and to retire, just like you had to learn to grow up." For me it was a learning process both times, and it was more than a little painful.

The Communication Trap

In chapter 5 we noted the fact that as couples grow older they tend to express less love and feel less affectionate toward one another. We believed a lack of deep and intimate communication was likely responsible for that frightening trend. There can be no doubt that every stage in life demands good communication. This is true in spades during the retirement years. Being underfoot, and around for lunch as well as breakfast and dinner, can so easily create an environment in which a couple take each other so for granted, that what is said and heard loses meaning and intensity.

More than once Harriett and I have been trapped in a misunderstanding because we've inadvertently expressed ourselves poorly or have not listened carefully. I'm sure there are a variety of reasons why this can happen, but I strongly suspect that we are guilty at times of hearing what we *want* to hear rather than what is really said and meant.

Harriett has come upon another possible reason for misunderstandings: "I recently read a small piece on a fascinating new theory. The article suggested that, scientifically, there is a vast difference between the innate thinking processes of women and men. Now, I don't know whether or not this theory will weather investigation, but I was attracted to the idea, because I have long felt that Floyd and I go at this thinking business in an entirely different way. Our difference may not be caused by gender, but then again, maybe it is."

As far as this theory goes, time will tell. But this we know for sure: while our culture and backgrounds have certain minor differences, for the most part there is a marked similarity in our heritage. Yet, our thinking procedures are, without question, vastly different. Being aware of this possibility has helped us a great deal, adding spice to our marriage and broadening our understanding of ourselves and others. Our love for one another keeps us continually alerted to the importance of what we say and how we say it. *Remember, words do make a difference*—especially to a lifetime married couple in the retirement years.

A Time for Learning and Doing

The sure formula for effective and enriching retirement years involves *continuing to discover, explore, and enjoy satisfying activities, both as individuals and as a couple.* We read somewhere that the retirement years offer the opportunity for a "reconversion" from earning a living and raising a family to creative self-development, including making a contribution to the welfare of our community and the world.

This can take as many forms as there are people. It can involve volunteer work on community projects, service with Habitat for Humanity, volunteer church work, studying a foreign language, taking courses in computer language and science, a planned reading program focused on both non-fiction and fiction, cooking and delivering Meals on Wheels. In short, *retirement frees us to express our vocation in new ways, to broaden our minds, and to make a difference through service to others.*

A myth that finds its way into print now and then is that by the time we're old enough to retire, we're not as sharp or creative as we once were. Nothing could be further from the truth, unless we've suffered from a crippling illness. Hugh Downs refers in his book to the example of Justice Oliver Wendell Holmes, Jr., who at age ninety-two was still active on the United States Supreme Court. It is said that one day Justice Holmes was found sitting in his library reading Plato—"to improve my mind," he said.

There are countless other examples that validate this truth. But the one that speaks most loudly to me is one of my literary heroes, James Michener. He wrote his first book, *Tales of the South Pacific,* a Pulitzer Prize winner, at age forty. He went on from there to produce a long list of best-sellers. He published his memoirs at eighty-five, and his latest novel, *Recessional,* was published when he was eighty-seven.

Now, it is true that not all of us can be like James Michener. But we all can be creative learners and doers, irrespective of age and income. Because of our particular interests, Harriett and I keep in close touch with several authors with whom we have worked in the book world over the years. As writers, we enjoy putting our thoughts and ideas in written form. In addition, we are both active volunteers in the work of our church, and we are avid readers; we each usually have two or three books going most of the time. These things work well for us and provide many useful and creative outlets.

A Time for Each Other

One of the potentially enriching rewards of the retirement years is the experience of having quality time for each other. We remember so well those earlier years of marriage that were jam-packed with establishing a home and raising children from the diaper stage through college. And throughout all of this there was the struggle for achievement in the marketplace and professional world.

Unfortunately, all too often a couple can become so absorbed in succeeding that the marriage relationship becomes a near casualty or drifts into a dull routine. The romance and the sizzle can wear so thin that the "once so much in love" couple just sort of put up with each other.

Throughout this book we've tried to honestly describe the earlier years of our marriage. And while we had wrestled with many of the same feelings and emotions experienced by any couple, we happily moved into our retirement life very much in love and eager for the new experiences that were ahead, in spite of our feelings of anxiety.

While neither of us has sacrificed our individual interests, we enjoy our time with other. As a matter of fact, I sort of over-did our togetherness in a few areas.

"He sure did! I discovered early on that Floyd had a weakness for grocery shopping. Now, I had done the grocery shopping during all of our earlier years together. But I soon discovered that Floyd was raring to go with me whenever the grocery list demanded attention. Well, that was all right, until I learned that he didn't think I was doing it right. For example, I like to go up and down every aisle and read the labels on the packaging. But Floyd was always hurrying me along. He wanted to shop his way, and I wanted to shop my way. It didn't turn out to be real "quality time" together on these shopping expeditions!

"Finally, we had a heart-to-heart talk in which I cleared the air about how I felt. I explained that I liked having him with me, but that I thought I'd done a pretty good job over the years, and I wanted to shop the way I always had."

I hadn't realized what I was doing, but when Harriett explained how she felt, it made sense. I set about trying to change my ways. The changes didn't happen all at once, but I began to improve bit by bit over time. Now I think I've learned to "finger" things and even read the labels as I push the cart along.

I know this comes across as being a little thing, but so often it's the little things that build up and make a relationship rocky. Years ago I clipped out these words of Richard Armour's, "In large things we are convivial; what causes the trouble is the trivial." Believe me, *there are no trivial things in our retired life together; every moment is quality time.*

Rooted Together

The retirement years are hand-holding years, a time for hugs, a time for saying "I love you." It is a time for affirming each other in countless ways: "That was a delicious dinner." "Your new jacket makes you look so handsome." "That dress looks great in all the right places." "I'm so glad we got married."

We never outgrow the need for affirmation from our loved ones. Norman Peale tells a story that illustrates our need for each other in a beautiful and descriptive way:

> The truth is, we all need supportive relationships. I once heard a lecture in which the speaker talked about the great redwood trees of California, those magnificent giants of the forest towering as much as three hundred feet in the air. "You'd think such tall trees would require very deep roots," the speaker said. "Actually, redwoods have a very shallow root system, designed to capture all the surface moisture possible. These roots spread out in all directions, and as a result, all the roots of all the trees in a redwood grove are intertwined. They are locked together so that when the wind blows or a storm strikes, all the trees support and sustain one another. That is why

you almost never see a redwood standing alone. They need one another to survive."[4]

Being creatively intertwined with each other in a loving, supportive way is, we believe, the secret of a lifetime marriage—including the retirement years.

How We Researched This Book

The research and writing for this book took place over a period of a little over three and one-half years—from January 1977 through June 1980. A general description of our procedure is outlined in the following paragraphs.

After formulating two sets of interview questions, one for couples married at least twenty years and still active in their relationship, and the other for persons who were divorced after a minimum of twenty years of marriage, we had the interview questions checked for style and psychological and sociological integrity.

Contact with persons willing to be interviewed was arranged through a network of professional people—psychologists, clergymen, psychiatrists, and marriage counselors. We then established contact with the prospective interviewees by both letter and telephone, and arrangements were made for the interviews. No one personally known to us was included in our structured interviews.

All interviews were held in the homes or apartments of the persons being interviewed with the exception of three, which were held in offices. The length of time involved was approximately two hours for interviews with divorced persons and three hours with married couples.

We held twenty-eight structured interviews with married couples and eighteen structured interviews with persons who were divorced. In addition, shorter unstructured interviews were held with thirty-two persons, and numerous extended conversations with other persons furnished input for our thinking.

The average age of the couples participating in our structured interviews was 53.16 years; the average number of years married was 31.11. All were high school graduates, and half of the persons had completed four years of college. Their income positioned them in the middle and upper-middle class range—from $15,000 to over $50,000 a year. Forty percent of the wives worked outside the home either part-time or full-time. All of the couples had children. Most were active to some degree in either church or synagogue.

The average age of divorced persons interviewed was 48.8 years. At the time of divorce or separation their average age was 44.4 years, and they had been married before separation or divorce an average of 22.7 years. Their educational patterns were quite similar to those of the still married couples. The lapse time between their separation or divorce and our interview ranged from six months to five years; however, four couples' divorces were not final. All but one had children, and none had remarried.

The general geographic breakdown for persons interviewed included the Southeast, Midwest, Southwest, and Pacific Coast areas in the United States. All lived in either an urban or suburban setting.

In addition to both the structured and unstructured interviews held with married and divorced persons, four structured and six unstructured interviews were held with people in the helping professions. These were for the purpose of assisting in the evaluation of our data and to contribute to the data already received.

The interview research and its analysis were completed in the summer of 1979, and the writing was finished in June 1980. Some revisions were made and a new chapter was written for the 1995 edition.

Questions to Think About

After Harriett and I had completed our full schedule of interviews, we set aside one day on a cross-country car trip to respond individually to the questions we had used, just as if someone else was interviewing us. We agreed to be as open and frank in our responses as the people we had interviewed had been with us. It was a stimulating and thought-provoking experience, and we felt better for having done it. Even after more than forty years of marriage at that time, we learned things about ourselves and each other that we hadn't known before. And that exercise has enriched and given further insight into our own relationship. In addition, each person we interviewed, in his or her own way, said that responding to the questions we raised caused them to think about their marriage relationship in a completely different way than ever before.

For this reason we are including the following questions here. While, of course, not every question will apply to everyone, we believe a thoughtful and considered response to them will be an enriching and growing experience to the individual reader, to couples going through them together, and to persons involved in group discussion and study.

A final word: the order of the questions is structured to maintain a certain rhythm. Because of the possible emotional heaviness of some of them, not every question on a related subject is asked at one time.

1. How would you describe yourself as a person? Do you think of yourself as being outgoing? Or as an introvert? Do you like yourself as a person? Are you inclined to be perfectionistic and over-demanding of yourself? Would you say that you have the ability to laugh at yourself? Do you see yourself as a person of very firm opinions—possibly a little dogmatic? Or do you see yourself as being quite flexible?

2. Do you enjoy your work? Or does the routine tend to become depressive?

3. What do you find to be most exciting or personally stimulating about your interests or experiences today?

4. How do you feel about the mood or health of society today? Are you happy with the political and social climate in our country?

5. The divorce rate in the United States today is the highest in the world. What are your observations as to the reasons for this?

6. In thinking back over your school years, which do you recall as being the happiest: grade school, junior high school, high school, college? Why?

7. How old were you when you first started to date?

8. How old were you when you first started dating your spouse?

9. How long did you date before getting married?

10. Was your courtship tranquil? Or was it stormy at times?

11. How old were you when you got married?

12. As you anticipated marriage, what three qualities attracted you to your prospective mate? Was there any one quality that irritated you?

13. What was the attitude of your parents to your serious dating? To your marriage?

14. Why did you want to get married? For convenience? A desire to leave home? Social pressure? Sexual attraction?

Loneliness? Love? Security? Escape from parental influence or domination?

15. How soon after your marriage did your children start to arrive? Were you ready to start a family at that time?

16. What does your mate do or say that really makes you feel good as a person? What does he (she) do to build you up and make you feel worthwhile? What kinds of things do you enjoy doing together? Are there any particular things your mate does which tend to not make you feel O.K. or worthwhile? How do you cope with these feelings?

17. How do you react to making decisions—little or big—on a day-to-day basis? Buying new furniture? Buying a new car? Buying a house? Moving from one place to another? Buying a painting?

18. As a couple, what is your pattern for making decisions? Do you feel that husband and wife should have equal authority in making decisions? Or should the husband have the final word?

19. As a person, how do you tend to handle crises? Try to ignore them? Postpone facing them? Get uptight?

20. What do you consider to be the major crisis in your married life?

21. As you reflect on your parents' marriage during your growing-up years, how would you describe it?

22. Do you feel that your parents' marriage has been a strong influence on your own attitude toward marriage?

23. In just a few sentences, how would you describe your father? Your mother?

24. What kind of a relationship did you have while growing up with your brothers and sisters? Has that relationship changed in your adult life?

25. In thinking about marriage as a young person, what did you expect it to be like? In what ways has your marriage differed from those early expectations?

Marriage for a Lifetime

26. How has your philosophy of marriage changed over the years?

27. To what extent have you had intimate relationships (not sexual) with persons of your own sex?

28. To what extent have you had intimate relationships (not sexual) with persons of the opposite sex?

29. Some people feel that while having children is a rewarding experience, the sense of satisfaction in marriage drops during the period one is raising them. Do you feel that raising children tends to put a strain on marriage? Is marital satisfaction reduced during those child-raising years?

30. During the early period of your marriage—say the first year or two—how did you usually cope with disagreements? Did you bury your feelings? Explode immediately? Sulk? What were the primary disagreements during this period?

31. Have these pressure points of disagreement changed over the years? If so, how? Has it become easier to cope, or more difficult?

32. Has the sense of satisfaction in your marriage changed in any way during the last ten years or so?

33. When you have disagreements now—strong differences of opinion—how do you usually express your anger? Who usually makes the first move toward reconciliation? As a rule, what kinds of words or actions usually trigger these arguments?

34. What kinds of things do you disagree strongly about today?

35. After all these years, what small or petty thing does your mate still do which irritates you?

36. How do you express criticism of your spouse?

37. Thinking back over the growing-up period in your parents' home, do you recall seeing and hearing outward verbal and nonverbal expressions of love and caring?

38. How would you describe the mood and climate of your home as a child? Were your parents strict? Permissive? What about touch? Do you recall being hugged?

39. As a child, were you built up and affirmed as a person? Was the philosophy in the home for children to "be seen and not heard"?

40. Do you find it fairly easy to develop caring relationships with other persons? In what ways are you able to express caring feelings toward others? How many intimate friends do you have with whom you can be reasonably open?

41. In your own marriage, do you find it easy or difficult to affirm or compliment your spouse?

42. Do you as a person find it easy or difficult to receive compliments? Do you feel uncomfortable when someone pays you a compliment?

43. Did you experience any particular health problems during the growing-up years?

44. Have there been any particular health problems over the years of your married life? Times of deep anxiety, or deep depression? If so, do you feel that these have affected your marriage relationship in any way?

45. Have you experienced any particular emotional problems over the years of your married life? Times of deep anxiety or deep depression? If so, do you feel that these have affected your marriage relationship in any way?

46. In your crowd as a young person, did you think then that your peers were having sexual relations before marriage? How did you react to this? Did you go along with it?

47. Were you sexually active before marriage? If so, how do you feel about that now?

48. How do you feel about the increasing acceptance in our culture of living together before marriage to determine compatibility?

49. Do you feel it is morally wrong for people who are not married to live together?

50. How would you rate the importance of a mutually satisfactory sex relationship to the success of marriage?

51. In your own experience, do you feel you were prepared to some degree, at least, for the sexual give and take and enjoyment at the time of your marriage?

52. How would you say your sexual relationship as a couple has changed over the years?

53. Were there certain periods during your marriage when this relationship seemed strained? How did you cope? Were you able to discuss this frankly with each other and share your deepest feelings?

54. There's a great deal more openness in the discussion of the sex relationship in marriage today. How do you feel about this?

55. Was it easy or difficult to discuss sex with your children?

56. In looking ahead, what are your dreams for the future?

57. Can you recall when you began to feel you were moving into the midlife stage?

58. How did you feel about moving into this new midlife stage? What kind of changes began to surface in your thinking and activities?

59. In reflecting on your movement into midlife or middle age, what do you feel are the most difficult problems you've had to face? What changes of attitude and lifestyle seem to be occurring? In general, do you find it easier to discuss these problems with each other than the ones which were a part of your earlier married years?

60. On a scale of 1 to 10, how do you rate your ability to cope with change? Do you find it more difficult now than when you were first married?

61. What career changes have you made during the period of your marriage? Do you feel that any such changes affected your marriage relationship?

62. Growth of one kind or another is inevitable in the human experience. How would you compare your rate and direction of growth with that of your spouse? Has your respective growth tended to draw you together or pull you apart?

63. Over the years, to what extent have you shared the same interests?

64. As a child, did you feel that your parents approved of you? Did you feel that you "measured up"? Do you think your parents approve of you now?

65. As a parent, how did you regard your children's place in the home? Were you strict or permissive with them?

66. Were you generally in agreement about disciplining your children?

67. Was it fairly easy or quite difficult for you to openly express your love for them in words and in physical ways such as hugging?

68. What is your relationship with your children now? And, if they are married, to their spouses? Do you approve of your adult children's lifestyle?

69. How important was religion in your childhood home? What are your earliest recollections of how you felt about God? How did your feelings change as a teenager?

70. Throughout the years of your own marriage, what role have religion and the church played in your own marriage and home life?

71. Have there been any changes in your attitude toward God and the church since you entered the midlife stage?

72. What are the primary sources from which you receive feelings of self-worth? Spouse? Job? Physical appearance?

Age? Money? Material possessions? Facility as a lover? Ability as an achiever?

73. In your marriage, who assumes the primary responsibility for handling the finances?

74. Are you able to freely discuss financial matters and concerns without becoming upset or angry?

75. What is your spouse's attitude toward money? How does this compare with your attitude? If there are differences, are they reconcilable or do they produce friction?

76. Who is the head of your household?

77. On a scale of 1 to 10, how would you rate in importance the idea that that which brings greatest happiness to you as a person should be the primary standard for your actions?

78. What do you think is the glue that has held your marriage together?

79. Was there a particular time when you wondered whether you would make it as a married couple?

80. Did you ever seriously consider separating, either on a trial basis or permanently?

81. Reflecting back, say, over the early years of your marriage, if you had the opportunity, how would you like to change your marriage?

82. In looking back over your entire married life to this point, what would you want to change about your marriage?

The following are additional questions we asked divorced persons.

83. Exactly how long has it been since your divorce was final?

84. Have you remarried? If so, how long after your divorce? How long have you been remarried?

85. How many years were you married before your separation and divorce?

86. How long before your actual separation and divorce did the idea first occur to you that this might happen?

87. In thinking back on your marriage, what did your former husband/wife do that made you feel good as a person? How did he/she make you feel worthwhile? What kinds of things did you really enjoy doing together?

88. What kinds of things did your former spouse do that made you feel not worthwhile? Or guilty?

89. As you reflect on your marriage, are there things you felt other couples had that you didn't have? Did you ever feel cheated in any way?

90. Your marriage lasted for ___ years; why do you think you stayed together as long as you did?

91. What kind of a price do you feel you paid to remain married as long as you did?

92. At the time the decision was made for you and your spouse to separate and get a divorce, was a third person involved with either of you? As time passed, did that third person remain important?

93. Who first expressed the desire for divorce? You? Your mate? If you did, what were your spouse's reactions? If your mate suggested divorce first, did you feel good about it? Feel disbelief? Feel anger?

94. Do you have happy or unhappy memories of your sex life during your marriage?

95. Would you say that there were times when either you or your spouse used sex in your relationship by withholding for bad behavior? By bestowing it in exchange for favors or gifts?

96. How would you characterize the sexual activity of your other divorced friends? What are your feelings about the sex choices or activities of a divorced person?

97. Have you been sexually active since your divorce?

98. What were your children's reactions when they learned that you were to be divorced?

99. How did you feel about your children's first reactions to your divorce?

100. Did you undergo any periods of trial separation prior to your final separation and divorce?

101. In looking back, is there anything you would want to change about your own part in your divorce?

102. Describe for us as honestly and vividly as possible your feelings during the divorce process. What were your feelings the day the divorce became final? What about the next six months? A year later?

103. How do you feel about your ex-spouse now? What is your present relationship?

104. As you reflect back from this perspective, have you at any time considered your divorce a mistake?

Notes

Chapter 1: What Ever Happened to Marriage?
1. Peter Drucker, *Age of Continuity* (New York: Harper and Row, 1969).

2. Paul C. Glick and Arthur J. Norton, "Marrying, Divorcing, and Living Together in the U.S. Today," *Population Bulletin*, vol. 32, no. 5 (Washington, DC: Population Reference Bureau, Inc., 1977), pp. 3–9. Quoted by courtesy of Population Reference Bureau, Inc.

3. Norval D. Glenn, *USA Today*, May 1993, p. 27.

4. Ibid.

5. James A. Peterson, *Married Love in the Middle Years* (New York: Association Press, 1968), p. 20.

6. Norval D. Glenn, p. 27.

7. Margaret Mead, *Culture and Commitment* (Garden City, NY: 1970), p. 79.

Chapter 2: Why Did You Get Married?
1. "Marriage Makes a Comeback," *Family Weekly*, December 31, 1978.

Chapter 3: What Did You Expect?
1. Mary Susan Miller, "Do Men and Women Expect the Same Things from Marriage?" *Family Weekly*, May 8, 1977.

2. Albert Lee and Carol Allman Lee, *The Total Couple* (Dayton, OH: Lorenz Press, 1977), p. 189.

3. Chuck Gallagher, S.J., *The Marriage Encounter* (New York: Bantam Books, 1975), p. 117.

4. Sheldon Vanauken, *A Severe Mercy* (New York: Harper and Row, 1977), p. 37.

5. Calvin S. Hall and Vernon J. Nordby, *A Primer of Jungian Psychology* (New York: New American Library, 1973), p. 32.

6. Alex Osborn, *Your Creative Power*, quoting Albert Batzer (New York: Dell Books, 1948).

7. Reuel L. Howe, *The Creative Years* (New York: Seabury Press, 1959), pp. 50–51.

8. Viktor E. Frankl, *Man's Search for Meaning* (Boston: Beacon Press, 1962), p. 72.

9. Sam Levenson, *You Don't Have to Be in Who's Who to Know What's What* (New York: Simon and Schuster, 1979), p. 28.

Chapter 4: What Is Commitment?

1. Dr. Wallace Denton, Professor of Family Studies and Director, Marriage and Family Counseling Center, Purdue University, in a letter to the authors dated September 6, 1979.

2. Kathy Lowry, "Marriage Makes a Comeback," *Family Weekly*, December 31, 1978.

3. Saul Pett, "Hubert Humphrey: The Old Warrior Faces Up to Another Crisis," *Dallas Morning News*, January 23, 1977.

4. Marilyn Hoffman, "Women's Movement Turns to Family, Mainstream America," *Christian Science Monitor*, reprinted in *The Arizona Republic* (Phoenix), December 17, 1979.

5. William H. Masters and Virginia E. Johnson in association with Robert J. Levin, *The Pleasure Bond* (Boston: Little, Brown & Co., 1970, 1971, 1972, 1973, 1974), pp. 251–252.

6. Eric Hoffer, *The Passionate State of Mind* (New York: Harper and Row, 1955), p. 60.

7. Chuck Gallagher, S.J., *The Marriage Encounter* (New York: Bantam Books, 1975), p. 119.

8. Viktor E. Frankl, *Man's Search for Meaning* (Boston: Beacon Press, 1962), p. 65.

9. Paul Tournier, *To Understand Each Other* (Atlanta: John Knox Press, 1967), p. 9.

10. Mark Twain, *The Adventures of Huckleberry Finn* (New York: Bantam Books, 1965), p. 4. A new amplified edition with special aids for understanding and enjoyment.

11. Peggy Stanton, *The Daniel Dilemma* (Waco, TX: Word, 1978), pp. 41–42.

12. Rollo, May, *Man's Search for Himself* (New York: New American Library, 1953), p. 206.

13. Alfred C. Kinsey, Wardell B. Pomeroy, and Clyde E. Martin, *Sexual Behavior in the Human Male* (Philadelphia: W.B. Saunders Co., 1948), p. 544.

14. Paul Tournier, *The Meaning of Persons* (New York: Harper and Row, 1957), p. 230.

15. Brian Moore, *The Luck of Ginger Coffee* (New York: Penguin Books, 1960), p. 202.

Chapter 5: Making Sure You Understand Each Other

1. Quoting Dr. Roy Rhodes in "Cheating" by Jeanna Sara Dorin, *Dallas Morning News,* May 28, 1978.

2. Dr. Bill Blackburn, given in a lecture, Dallas, Texas.

3. Jessie Bernard, "Development Tasks of the NCFR—1963–1988," *Journal of Marriage and Family* 16 (February 1964), pp. 33–34.

4. Chuck Gallagher, S.J., *The Marriage Encounter* (New York: Doubleday, 1975), p. 117, Bantam.

5. William H. Masters and Virginia E. Johnson in association with Robert J. Levin, *The Pleasure Bond* (Boston: Little, Brown & Co., 1970, 1971, 1972, 1973, 1974), p. 229.

6. Don Fabun, *Communication: The Transfer of Meaning* (Beverly Hills, CA: Glencoe Press, 1968), p. 10.

7. W. Somerset Maugham, *The Razor's Edge* (Garden City, NY: International Collector's Library, 1944), p. 3.

8. Fabun, *Communication*, p. 42.

9. Clifford H. Swensen, Jr., "How Long Does Love Last?" *Family Weekly,* July 22, 1979.

10. Saul Gellerman, *Management by Motivation* (AMA, 1968), p. 46.

11. Jesse S. Nirenberg, *Getting Through to People* (Englewood Cliffs, NJ: Prentice-Hall, 1963), p. 14.

12. Robert R. Ball, *The "I Feel" Formula* (Waco, TX: Word Books, 1977), pp. 9–17.

13. Masters and Johnson, *The Pleasure Bond*, p. 94.

14. Sven Wahlroos, *Family Communication—A Guide to Emotional Health* (New York: Macmillan Co., 1974), p. 214.

15. Paul Tournier, *To Understand Each Other* (Atlanta: John Knox Press, 1967), p. 8.

16. Gallagher, *The Marriage Encounter*, p. 69.

17. Reuel L. Howe, *The Miracle of Dialogue* (New York: Seabury Press, 1963), p. 39.

18. Tournier, *To Understand Each Other*, p. 31
19. Howe, *The Miracle of Dialogue*, p. 3.

Chapter 6: Communicating without Words
1. John Faul and David Augsburger, *Beyond Assertiveness* (Waco, TX: Word Books, 1980).
2. Terry Hekker, *Ever Since Adam and Eve* (New York: William Morrow and Co., 1979), p. 121.
3. John Powell, *Why Am I Afraid to Tell You Who I Am?* (Niles, IL: Argus Communications, 1969), pp. 157–158.
4. Reuel L. Howe, *The Creative Years* (New York: Seabury Press, 1959), p. 37.
5. Dorothy T. Samuel, *Fun and Games in Marriage* (Waco, TX: Word Books, 1973), p. 16.
6. Max Luscher, *The Luscher Color Test*, trans. and ed. Ian A. Scott (New York: Pocket Books, 1969), p. 12.

Chapter 7: The Adventure of Growing Together
1. Gail Sheehy, *Passages* (New York: E. P. Dutton Co., 1976), p. 353.
2. William H. Masters and Virginia E. Johnson in association with Robert J. Levin, *The Pleasure Bond* (Boston: Little, Brown & Co., 1970, 1971, 1972, 1973, 1974), p. 37.
3. Daniel J. Levinson, *The Seasons of a Man's Life* (New York: Ballantine Books, 1978), p. 21.
4. Ibid.
5. Harold C. Lyon, Jr., *Tenderness Is Strength* (New York: Harper and Row, 1977), p. 104.
6. Levinson, *The Seasons of a Man's Life*, p. 18.
7. Clifford H. Swenson, Jr., "Marriages that Endure" by Charlotte D. Moore in *Families Today*, Vol. 1, Eunice Corfman, ed. (Rockville, MD: National Institute of Mental Health, 1980), p. 250.
8. Bruce Larson, *The Meaning and Mystery of Being Human* (Waco, TX: Word Books, 1978), pp. 69–70.
9. Jack Balswick, *Why I Can't Say I Love You* (Waco, TX: Word Books, 1978), pp. 9–10.
10. Masters and Johnson, *The Pleasure Bond*, p. 37.
11. Paul Tournier, *The Adventure of Living* (New York: Harper and Row, 1965), p. 67.

12. James A. Peterson, *Married Love in the Middle Years* (New York: Association Press, 1968), p. 15.

13. Lyon, *Tenderness Is Strength*, p. 10.

14. Carl Rogers, *On Becoming a Person* (Boston: Houghton and Mifflin, 1961), p. 116.

15. Paul Tournier, *To Understand Each Other* (Atlanta: John Knox Press, 1967), p. 34.

16. Gay Talese, "Stronger Marriages," *Family Weekly*, December 30, 1979.

17. Rollo May, *Man's Search for Himself* (New York: New American Library, 1953), p. 69.

Chapter 8: Surviving the Child-Rearing Years

1. Hans Selye, *Stress Without Distress* (Philadelphia: J.B. Lippincott, 1974), p. 67.

2. Ibid., p. 34.

3. Robert O. Blood, Jr., *Marriage* (New York: Free Press, 1969), p. 438.

4. Ibid., p. 439.

5. Evelyn Millis Duvall, *Family Development* (Philadelphia: J.B. Lippincott, 1971), p. 231.

6. Quoted from a lecture given by George Gallup, Jr. to the Seminar on the Family, April 1979, sponsored by the Christian Life Commission, Southern Baptist Convention.

7. Richard Farson, a psychologist and father of five, in an interview in *Human Behavior*, July 1976.

8. Duvall, *Family Development*, p. 101.

9. Glenn D. Norval, *USA Today*, May 1993.

10. Richard Flaste, "Children Place Strain on Marriage Partners," *New York Times* News Service, 1977.

11. Eunice Corfman, ed., *Families Today*, vol. 1, "Parents as Leaders: The Role of Control and Discipline"; principal investigator: Diana Baumrind, Ph.D.; author: Herbert Yahraes (Rockville, MD: U.S. Department of Health, Education and Welfare, 1980), pp. 291, 297.

12. Henri J. M. Nouwen, *Reaching Out* (New York: Doubleday, 1975), p. 58.

13. James T. Fisher and Lowell S. Hawley, *A Few Buttons Missing* (Philadelphia: J.B. Lippincott, 1951), pp. 125–26.

Chapter 9: The Twin Stresses of Money and Work

1. Letha Scanzoni and John Scanzoni, *Men, Women and Change—A Sociology of Marriage and Family* (New York: McGraw-Hill, 1976), pp. 336–37.

2. Robert O. Blood, Jr., *Marriage* (New York: Free Press, 1969), p. 239.

3. Carol Craft, "A Taboo Topic? Marital Money Talk Urged by Economist," *Waco Tribune-Herald,* May 12, 1980.

4. Daniel J. Levinson, *The Seasons of a Man's Life* (New York: Ballantine Books, 1978), p. 9.

5. Wayne E. Oates, *Confessions of a Workaholic* (Nashville: Abingdon Press, 1971), p. 4.

6. Denise D. Turner, "How to Stop Believing," *Your Church,* March-April, 1980.

7. Ted W. Engstrom and David J. Juroe, *The Work Trap* (Old Tappan, NJ: Fleming H. Revell, 1979), p. 102.

8. Ibid., p. 101.

9. Evelyn Mills Duvall, *Family Development* (Philadelphia: J.B. Lippincott, 1971), pp. 177–78.

Chapter 10: The Best Half of Life?

1. Gail Sheehy, *Passages* (New York: E.P. Dutton, Co., 1976), p. 337.

2. Henry Still, *Surviving the Male Mid-Life Crisis* (New York: Thomas Y. Crowell Co., 1977), p. 9.

3. C. G. Jung, *Modern Man in Search of a Soul* (New York: Harcourt Brace Jovanovich, 1933), p. 108.

4. Reuel L. Howe, *The Creative Years* (New York: Seabury Press, 1959), p. 43.

5. *The Royal Bank of Canada Monthly Letter,* vol. 51, no. 4, April 1970.

6. Nancy Mayer, *The Male Mid-Life Crisis* (New York: Doubleday, 1978), p. 219.

7. Kate White, "The Cronkites: That's the Way it Is," *Family Weekly,* February 10, 1980.

8. Robert J. Havighurst, "Middle Age—The New Prime of Life" in *Aging in Today's Society,* ed. Clark Tibbitts and Wilma Donahue (Englewood Cliffs, NJ: Prentice-Hall, 1960), p. 137.

9. Judd Marmor, "The Defense of Masters and Johnson," *World Magazine,* January 30, 1973, pp. 24–27.

10. Bernice Neugarten and others, *Personality in Middle and Late Life* (New York: Atherton Press, 1964).

11. Eric Hoffer, *The Passionate State of Mind* (New York: Harper and Row, 1954), p. 97.

12. Judson T. and Mary G. Landis, *Building a Successful Marriage*, 4th ed. (Englewood Cliffs, NJ: Prentice-Hall, 1963), pp. 351, 352.

13. Robert A. Raines, *Lord, Could You Make It a Little Better?* (Waco, TX: Word Books, 1972), p. 135.

Chapter 11: Marriage and Retirement

1. Avis D. Carlson, *In the Fullness of Time* (Chicago: Contemporary Books, Inc., 1977), p. 15.

2. The Royal Bank of Canada Monthly Letter, vol. 53, no. 3, March 1972.

3. Hugh Downs and Richard J. Roll, *The Best Years Book: How to Plan for Fulfillment, Security, and Happiness in the Retirement Years* (New York: Delacorte Press/Eleanor Friede, 1981), p. 2.

4. Norman Vincent Peale, *Positive Imaging* (Pawling, N.Y.: Foundation for Christian Living, 1982), p. 78.

Suggested Reading

Abrahamsen, David. *The Road to Emotional Maturity*. Englewood Cliffs, NJ: Prentice-Hall, 1958.

Alexander, Zane. *Till Death Do Us Part*. Philadelphia: Westminster Press, 1976.

Arnold, William V., Dixie McKie Baird, Joan Trigg Langan, and Elizabeth Blakemore Vaughan. *Divorce: Prevention or Survival*. Philadelphia: Westminster Press, 1977.

Augsburger, David W. *Cherishable: Love and Marriage*. New York: William Morrow and Co., 1969.

Bach, George R. and Peter Wyden. *The Intimate Enemy*. New York: William Morrow and Co., 1969.

Blood, Robert, O. Jr. *Marriage*. New York: Free Press, 1969.

Clinebell, Howard J. and Charlotte H. Clinebell. *The Intimate Marriage*. New York: Harper and Row, 1970.

Conway, Jim. *Men in Mid-Life Crisis*. Elgin, IL: David C. Cook, 1978.

Corfman, Eunice, ed. *Families Today*. Vol. 1. Rockville, MD: U.S. Department of Health, Education and Welfare, National Institute of Mental Health, 1980.

Davitz, Joel and Lois Davitz. *Making It from 40 to 50*. New York: Random House, 1976.

Duvall, Evelyn Millis. *Family Development*. Philadelphia: J.B. Lippincott, 1971.

Engstrom, Ted W. and David J. Juroe. *The Work Trap*. Old Tappan, NJ: Fleming H. Revell, 1979.

Epstein, Joseph. *Divorced in America*. New York: Penguin Books, 1974.

Fabun, Don. *Communication: The Transfer of Meaning*. Beverly Hills, CA: Glencoe Press, 1968.

Faul, John and David Augsburger. *Beyond Assertiveness*. Waco, TX: Word Books, 1980.

Gallagher, Chuck, S.J. *The Marriage Encounter*. New York: Bantam Books, 1975.

Hallberg, Edmond C. *The Gray Itch*. New York: Warner Books, 1977.

Hekker, Terry. *Ever Since Adam and Eve*. New York: William Morrow and Co., 1979.

Howe, Reuel L. *The Creative Years*. New York: Seabury Press, 1959.

―――. *The Miracle of Dialogue*. New York: Seabury Press, 1963.

Jung, C.G. *Modern Man in Search of a Soul*. New York: Harcourt Brace Jovanovich, 1933.

Kilgore, James E. *Try Marriage Before Divorce*. Waco, TX: Word Books, 1978.

Kinsey, Alfred C., Wardell B. Pomeroy, and Clyde E. Martin. *Sexual Behavior in the Human Male*. Philadelphia: W.B. Saunders Co., 1948.

Koile, Earl. *Listening as a Way of Becoming*. Waco, TX: Word Books, 1977.

Krantzler, Mel. *Creative Divorce*. New York: New American Library, 1974.

Landis, Judson T. and Mary G. Landis. *Building a Successful Marriage*. 4th ed. Englewood Cliffs, NJ: Prentice-Hall, Inc., 1963.

Lee, Albert and Carol Allman Lee. *The Total Couple*. Dayton, OH: Lorenz Press, 1977.

Levinson, Daniel J. *The Seasons of a Man's Life*. New York: Ballantine Books, 1978.

Lyon, Harold C., Jr. *Tenderness Is Strength*. New York: Harper and Row, 1977.

Mace, David and Vera Mace. *Marriage Enrichment in the Church*. Nashville: Broadman Press, 1976.

Masters, William H. and Virginia E. Johnson in association with Robert J. Levin. *The Pleasure Bond*. Boston: Little, Brown & Co., 1970, 1971, 1972, 1974.

May, Rollo. *Man's Search for Himself*. New York: New American Library, 1953.

Mayer, Nancy. *The Male Mid-Life Crisis*. Garden City, NY: Doubleday, 1978.

Neugarten, Bernice et al. *Personality in Middle and Late Life*. New York: Atherton Press, 1964.

Nirenberg, Jesse S. *Getting Through to People*. Englewood Cliffs, NJ: Prentice-Hall, 1963.

Oates, Wayne E. *Confessions of a Workaholic*. Nashville: Abingdon Press, 1971.

Peterson, James A. *Married Love in the Middle Years*. New York: Association Press, 1968.

Poticha, Joseph, M.D., with Art Southwood. *Use It or Lose It*. New York: Richard Marek, 1978.

Powell, John. *Why Am I Afraid to Tell You Who I Am?* Niles, IL: Argus Communications, 1969.

Puner, Morton. *Getting the Most Out of Your Fifties*. New York: Crown Publishers, 1977.

Rogers, Carl. *On Becoming a Person*. Boston: Houghton and Mifflin, 1961.

Sammons, David. *The Marriage Option*. Boston: Beacon Press, 1977.

Scanzoni, Letha and John Scanzoni. *Men, Women and Change—A Sociology of Marriage and Family*. New York: McGraw-Hill, 1976.

Selye, Hans. *Stress Without Distress*. Philadelphia: J.B. Lippincott, 1974.

Shedd, Charlie W. *Letters to Karen: On Keeping Love in Marriage*. Nashville: Abingdon Press, 1965.

——. *You Can Be a Great Parent*. Waco, TX: Word Books, 1970.

Sheehy, Gail. *Passages*. New York: E.P. Dutton Co., 1976.

Still, Henry. *Surviving the Male Mid-Life Crisis*. New York: Thomas Y. Crowell Co., 1977.

Tournier, Paul. *The Adventure of Living*. New York: Harper and Row, 1965.

——. *The Meaning of Persons*. New York: Harper and Row, 1957.

——. *To Understand Each Other*. Atlanta: John Knox Press, 1967.

Viscott, David, M.D. *How to Live with Another Person*. New York: Arbor House, 1974.

Wahlroos, Sven. *Family Communication—A Guide to Emotional Health*. New York: Macmillan Co., 1974.